The GURU who
ROCKED my LIFE!

A MYSTERIOUS TALE FILLED WITH POWERFUL CONCEPTS FOR LEADING AN AMAZING LIFE!

Vishnu Sharma

PARTRIDGE
A Penguin Random House Company

To order additional copies of this book, contact
Partridge India
000 800 10062 62
www.partridgepublishing.com/india
orders.india@partridgepublishing.com

This book is dedicated to my dad

CONTENTS

A Word From The Author

Dear Reader,

Congratulations! I am extremely happy that you have started your journey towards leading an exceptional life. Thank you for choosing this book. I have put my sincere effort to create this work and help you take a giant leap on your path towards destiny. I have embedded all the powerful concepts that will help you dwell into your inner world and bring about a change inside, so that you see the world changing outside to give you what you want. I am a spiritual seeker. I have been doing a lot of research on this subject which I love. This work is a gist of the wisdom that I have gained and the change that I have experienced on my own spiritual journey. There is nothing in this world that you cannot accomplish. My vision of life is to inspire you to realize your dreams and experience REAL HAPPINESS.

I believe that your experience with this book will change your life forever.

Have an amazing life ahead. Live your PURPOSE.

THE WORLD IS WAITING FOR YOUR EXPRESSION. Live GREAT!!

Vishnu Sharma

PREFACE

$\mathbf{W}$hat does LIFE mean to you? What is the definition of life from your perspective? Most of us would have not thought of writing a definition for Life. The reason for not defining is not that we cannot, but, we did not think of. We have learnt the meaning of thousands of complicated words in our school days, but we never thought of learning the meaning of the simple word which defines our existence—Life. The truth is that, there cannot be a single meaning which is common for all. Each one of us has our own definition of Life. Our life is ONLY OUR life. How can someone else give a meaning or definition for it?

The real need that exists today is to find your own definition. To define YOU. To find your own path to live in accordance to the definition; this can be written ONLY by YOU.

We all have heard people saying, "We have only one life. We have to live it to the fullest." I want you to understand the deeper meaning of this statement. What does this statement really mean? What does living fully mean to you? That is what most of us fail to understand. Without understanding the deeper meaning of that statement, whatever we try to do would be superficial living.

The deeper meaning lies in your own unique definition of LIFE. The real meaning of living life is in your own definition of YOU. That is when you live deeply. That is when you live life to the fullest. That is when you live with HAPPINESS. REAL happiness!

I want you all to make a deep commitment NOW that you are going to LIVE life to the fullest in the real sense. I want you to start working today, with utmost sincerity, to find your definition of life. I want you to put your complete effort in defining YOU in your own terms.

The purpose of this book is to help you in all your efforts. This story is of a young man like most of us. It is structured in a way that it will help peel the layers built by you over the REAL YOU who is deep inside.

All the best for your mysterious journey into yourself . . .

THE HAPPENSTANCE

It was time to leave. Lot of preparation went in explaining my five year old son that I would not be in town for the next three days. Hugged and kissed Simone and Aarav. Simone, the love of my life is the best thing that happened to me—she's amazing. During the departure, there was a strange feeling inside. I could not understand why. Deciding to analyze it later, I said bye and left for the airport. I flew to Chennai, the capital city of Tamil Nadu, a state in southern part of India.

I took a taxi from the airport to the bus stop. It was a forty five minute journey. Images of incidents over the last two days filled my mind. My aunt's call on my uncle's health condition, my struggle in office to get leave from work for three days, convincing Simone and Aarav in postponing the weekend beach plan and finally the strange feeling I had when I said bye to my wife and son. I was missing them like never before. It was for many days that my son asked me to take him to the beach. He loves to build sand castles. The promise of taking Aarav to beach was broken more than ten times. Sometimes because of Simone and many a time it was because of me. This time, we had cancelled all the other tasks and were one hundred percent sure to go. It is a great joy to see him build castles. Simone and I love watching the sea and just being there with each other. Leave alone the beach; it was a long time that we went out somewhere together. This feeling of guilt was what was troubling me. Last thing that I expected was a call from my aunt. I sincerely made another promise to myself that, on my return, we are going beach, come what may.

"Sir, we reached the bus stop", said the taxi driver.

"Thank you so much". I paid him, took my back pack and entered the bus stop. It was more than ten years that I travelled by bus. Thanks to the job I do and the assignments I get to do. I had been away from simple things like these. Even when I travelled with Simone and Aarav, we used to take a flight. We stayed in India till I was seventeen. Dad used to take me in bus to my granny's house. She lived in a far-off village. Bus was the only option to reach her place. My dad was a person with a great attitude. He was an amazing father. This I realized, after I became one.

"Selam . . . Selam", shouted the bus driver, to ensure that no one misses it. If anyone missed it, they could travel only in the next bus which was 2 hours later. I got in.

Shikar John. That's my name. We stayed in Northern California, United States. I worked in a giant software firm in the Silicon Valley. Simone worked as a teacher in a primary school. We led a very busy life. Aarav was in the same school where Simone worked. I have been working for last 15 years and my life was completely occupied with work, work and work. I could hardly spend a couple of hours even during the weekends with Simone and Aarav.

My aunt called around 9'o clock on Friday night.

"It has increased and spread across the body now. Yesterday our neighbor Neola aunty said that there is a treatment available. A well-known ancient Ayurvedic center in a place called Semmedu in Tamil Nadu has a medicine for it. Your uncle is not able to tolerate the pain. I spoke to a person at the center and informed that someone from our side will come and collect the medicine this Sunday. My son, I will not be able to travel leaving your Uncle alone. Can you please go and get that medicine for your uncle?"

Something which I could not deny. My uncle had a rare skin disease. He had red patches on his skin which were seen occasionally on few parts of his body. Doctors could not diagnose what it was. However the patches used to disappear after 2 to 3 days. As his age increased, we observed that both the frequency and the duration of these occurrences increased. He felt terrible pain in the area where the patches showed up. I decided to go.

It was Sunday Morning. Chennai was a hot place. The bus started to move. I felt nice as fresh breeze entered the bus. As we moved out of the city, I felt much better.

I heard of the Ayurveda during my childhood. My granny gave us a homemade medicine prepared using some Indian spices whenever I caught cold. Magically it worked every time I took it. She would tell me that it is an Ayurvedic medicine. Ayurveda is an age old powerful healing technique followed in India. All the images of my childhood and time with my granny ran past my mind as I was travelling in the bus. She was full of life lessons and adventurous stories.

We reached the place called Selam. I had to take a taxi from Selam to Semmedu. Completed my breakfast in a hotel and took a taxi. It was 9' o clock in the morning when I left from Selam. It was supposed to be a 2 and half hour drive.

We neared Kollimalai, the hill range where Semmedu was located. I was awestruck by the beauty. I opened the windows asking the driver to switch off the air conditioner. I felt very refreshing just by the silence and the purity of the air in those hills. I was feeling one with the nature and felt a sense of belonging to that place. I never looked at my watch. I felt that time stopped and filled me with stillness and peace. I was in tremendous joy just by being there looking at the mountains, enjoying the nature, as we drove up the hill.

"We reached Semmedu sir. This is the nearest hotel to the place you mentioned sir", said the driver as he dropped me in a hotel which was close to the Ayurveda center. I paid him and took his number to call him once I am done with my work.

There was an inordinate feeling within me as I placed my foot amidst the mountains and the tall trees which almost reached the sky. I was feeling home, though I was thousands of miles away. I checked into the hotel which was decent enough. After enquiring the receptionist, I walked in the direction towards the Ayurveda Center. It was approximately one mile from the hotel. I did not want to take rest at the hotel. I started immediately as I wanted to finish the task and return home that night.

As I walked towards the Ayurveda center, I was looking at the trees and mountains around. I felt that they were talking to me. As if they are closely related to me. I was breathing slowly and deeply and was feeling serene. There was immense energy filled in me because of the miraculous power I felt in the air. I walked slowly, wondering if this place was really on the earth that we are living now. Just thinking about the Tuesday, on which I had to resume my usual routine, created a lot of disturbance in me. It's so different. I was feeling that I was with myself after many days. Or maybe years. I was blessed to be there. I wanted to bring Simone there one day.

"Namaste", greeted a person at the entrance of the Ayurveda Center. Realizing that I did not understand the local language, he spoke to me in English. "Whom do you want to meet?"

I took out the bit of paper on which I had noted down the name. I read "Mr. Pundit Ram Rajan". The man stood still and calm. He was so composed while he said,

"I am sorry Sir. Pundit is out of village. He will return on Tuesday morning at 5'o clock. You can meet him on Tuesday evening at 4 PM."

"We called to inform that we are coming to collect a medicine for my uncle", I got really annoyed. "And we were confirmed that Mr. Pundit will be available to provide the medicine".

"I am sorry Sir. I do not know", is all what he said to me and went inside calmly. I was shocked and puzzled. I did not know what to do. Should I stay back or leave the place? I sat there on a small platform to think.

Suppose I go back, the very purpose of my travel to that place which is helping my uncle would not be met. If I stay, what's the guarantee that the person would return on Tuesday morning. My little son would be waiting for me. I did not have a clear answer. So I called Simone.

"Don't worry dear. Just stay back and complete the task. Aarav is fine and I will prepare him. You please take care", Simone said. I realized once again that I am incomplete without Simone. I love her so much.

Being relieved after talking to Simone, I started walking back to the hotel. It was 5:30 PM. As I was walked, I saw a many trails which were leading into the mountains. After the turbulence for a while, tranquility filled my mind again. I was a trekker in my college days. Memories of those days brought back the energy in me as I walked past the trails.

Trails were the key to any trek. My mind was getting heaved to the trail.

Half the way towards the hotel, I found a trail. Just after I passed the trail, I stumbled and fell down. There were minimal scratches on my right elbow. Those were very common during treks. I got up and wiped the dust. I looked at that trail again. I felt it was inviting me to take it up. I got tempted to go for it. Guess what? I did go for it . . . It was 5.45 PM.

As I followed the trail, the trees got denser and I was hearing birds chirping and singing. Those melodies, I had not heard that for more than a decade. I continued walking along the trail and it led me to something really astonishing. I reached a beautiful view point on the mountains. Gifted I was, is what I felt when I saw the beautiful sunset as I turned. The sun would drown into the mountains in few minutes. As I was looking at that beauty in serenity, I remembered what my father said-

"Son, our life is like the motion of the sun. It rises slowly and shines the most during the mid-day and slowly sets in the evening. The same way we do little in our early age and do whatever we aspire and shine during most of our middle age and finally lower the intensity of our contribution and finally go away. What do you think?"

"Yes dad! I agree with you", I said. "You are missing something my boy", he continued, "The sun never stops shining. When it sets for one side of the world, it serves the other. Moreover, it gives its light to the moon, which reflects the sun's light after it has gone for the day. In the same way, even after we go, our soul never goes anywhere. The body may go but the soul is always there and leaves its imprint".

My dad was a great man. He worked as a manager in the mining section of a big multinational cement making company. He was known for his sincerity and hard work. He brought me up with his values. Having planned well for his family which included me and my mother, he saved for my education and made me an engineer. He took good care of us and never worried about his own health. Having succeeded in bringing up a son of great values, what he failed in was to live his own dream. He was a great writer. In my school days many children visited our house for getting his poems and songs, which they sang in singing competitions at school. He worked only to earn for us. He kept his dream on hold and wanted to pursue it after his retirement. Life's basic principle of uncertainty took over and his life ended in less than a year after his retirement.

"It's getting dark my dear boy. Why don't you get back to your hotel", I heard a powerful yet sober voice at my back. "I think you should go now".

I got very scared when I heard that voice in those silence filled mountains. As I turned back, I saw a man in a black robe. He had sparkling sharp eyes. He looked very peaceful and unruffled. His vibes filled that space with more serenity and positive energy. He was calm and had a gentle smile on his face.

"Who are you sir?" I asked "Are you from this place or a visitor just like me?"

"People call me the Guru", he said, "I live here in that hut you can see on your right. So, did you decide to stay or go back to your place? Did the person in the Ayurveda center promise that he will give you the medicine you came for?"

I was shocked at his question. "How do you know about this?" I asked him, "Do you work at the Ayurveda Center?" He just smiled and said, "I admire your decision to stay back to support your uncle's health". I was bewildered and also getting scared at the same time. I repeated, "Who are you?"

"It does not really matter my boy. Whoever I am, it will not make any difference for you. You are in need of help and I am here to help you."

"I am not in need of any help. I came here only for my uncle's medicine. I will be leaving once I collect it. I really do not know who you are and I am leaving to my hotel right now" I said as I got more irate.

"My boy, if you are here for your uncle's medicine, why is that you are here, so far from your hotel? Why is that you are thinking of your dad?"

I got anxious and pleaded him, "Please tell me who you are and how do you know so many things about me?"

"As I said earlier, I am here to help you my boy. It does not really matter who I am, as long as I can support you with the help you need."

"But I can't stand this trepidation. If I need any help at this point of time, it is to know who you are. Please help me now," I replied vulnerably.

"Sure my son. If you really want to know who I am, I insist that you do something I want you to do."

"Please go ahead and tell me what I should do."

"For the next three days, you should spend some time with me. You should meet me at 6 AM every day. Remember that you should be here with your full commitment, or else you will be at loss. I want you be really sincere and adhere to what I say."

"This is ridiculous. Why should I meet you every day? It's ok even if I do not know who you are. I am leaving for now and I will never be back here again"

"I will wait here tomorrow morning at 6 AM. I wait here to help you, Shikar John", said that man with the same serene smile as I started walking away.

I never told him my name.

I was lying on my bed in the hotel room. I chose not to have dinner that night. Just gazing at the ceiling, I thought, "Who is this man? How does he know so much about me? Is he really here to help me? But I don't really need any help. I am a happy man with a lovely family and decent job, which pays me for more than a simple living. I have a good plan in place to have a secure future. Then, what is left for this man to help me with? He looks like a sage with nothing left for himself."

I tried to sleep after deciding not to go.

I could not sleep as my mind was still clinging to that Guru guy. I closed my eyes under duress. It was 5 AM, when I woke up. I saw the clock and got out of the bed. Inadvertently I was out of the hotel and on my way to the Guru's hut.

Day 1:
THE DISCOVERY

I walked slowly as I was still in the state of a dilemma. I was not sure. Am I doing the right thing or am I taking a risk that would cost me something that I can't afford? I felt that the turbulence within me was disturbing the stillness in those peaceful mountains. I could feel that the birds were cursing me for the vibes of turmoil which was affecting the serenity of their home.

"My son, I want share a small story with you," my dad once said to me when I was 18 and he was around 50 years old. "There was man in a village. He had an amazing son and a beautiful wife. The man loved his family very much. He worked day and night cutting wood in the forest and selling them to the carpenters in the city, which was 20 miles away from his village. One day when the wood cutter was on his way to the city to deliver his efforts, he started thinking of his childhood. He always wanted to be on the product side of his work. He wanted to do amazing carvings out of the wood. He wanted to create splendid designs.

One day during his child hood the wood-cutter shared this dream with his father. His father who was also a wood-cutter told him, "My son, we are wood cutters. Carving wood is not our work. Our forefathers have worked hard and earned a great name. We should follow them."

"But father, I love carving wood. Please allow me to do it. I am sure I will work very hard and earn a great name that would last for generations and also a good livelihood for us."

The wood cutter's father got angry and was not interested to continue the conversation. To end it he said, "First you earn money to serve you and your family. Save the money sufficient enough to buy a shop and also the wood sufficient enough to carve for ten years. Then you can go ahead and do what you want."

There was a long silence and no more discussion on that topic.

As usual, one fine day the wood cutter went to the city to sell his wood. He met a middle aged man at the wood carving shop. There were beautiful carvings that were placed in the display area. The wood cutter was amazed seeing the beauty of the carvings. He admired the immense effort and talent of the man who carved them. The man asked the boy, "Do you want to learn wood carving? I will teach you and you can be my assistant". The wood cutter was filled with joy. He told the man that he will come from the next day and walked backed happily to his village. He met his father and shared this happiest news.

His father said, "My son, it is big risk. Do you remember what I said when we discussed this topic last time? We are wood cutters and we need to have enough money before we get into these things."

The wood cutter was very sad as he could not say no to his father. He did not turn up to the man who promised him to teach the carving.

He started to save money so that one day he can save all that was required according to his father's list. Days, months and years passed, but he could barely save a minor part of what was required. As years passed, even his dream faded and finally vanished. He had a family and was earning sufficient for his livelihood. He led a content life. For few initial years, his dream surfaced whenever he saw the wood carver who had knocked his door of opportunity to live his dream. Over years, even that did not occur and he just smiled as he saw the man and moved on."

I hit the trail, where I had to take a turn to the Guru's hut. I walked faster as it was nearing 6 AM.

I reached the place finally and stood at the spot where I met Guru the previous day. I was still not sure about the risk I was getting into. At the same time, I felt that this mysterious guy really had something for me. I affirmed to myself that I was doing the right thing.

As I turned around, I found him sitting on a big rock. He was facing the sun, closing his eyes and sitting in a crossed leg position. I went nearer to him.

"Good morning Shikar. I knew you would come", he said still closing his eyes.

"How do you know that I am here, even while your eyes are closed?"

He just smiled and gently opened his eyes. His eye lids opened as if they were under complete control of their owner. His sparkling eyes were filled with amazing energy and I felt as if they were speaking to me even while he was silent. It was a divine moment.

"Who are you?" I asked again.

Ignoring my question, he said," You have to give me another commitment, my son".

"I told that I would meet you and 6 AM sharp, I was here. I kept my promise. What else do you want me to commit?"

"My boy, please remember, I asked you to spend time with me for the next three days. It's not about just the meeting. I will be able to help you only if you are here with me for few hours over next three days."

"Oh my God! Are you crazy? I will not spend any time with you. I already told you that I do not need any help. I just wanted to know who you are. Now, I don't even find the need for that. I will leave now."

As I said these words, I started moving from that place.

"Don't become another wood cutter", uttered the Guru.

I stood still. I was mystified yet another time.

"Abraham John was a great man. He had a number of inspiring stories to tell. Unfortunately, his own story ended at the brink of being an inspiring one", said the Guru.

I was baffled, "How do you my father? How do you know what I was thinking of?"

"My son, as I said, people call me the Guru, meaning—a teacher. A teacher knows everything about his student."

"Tell me what I should commit", I asked.

"You have to follow and practice whatever I tell you during these three days."

"Ok, I will".

"Life is a derivative of coincidences, my boy. Each and every event in any moment plays a role in what you are and what you become. And each event is the choice that we make at that moment. Our life is full of choice. If the wood cutter had chosen to live his dream, that moment of choice would have carved him into a new and different individual altogether. I am happy that you have chosen at this moment, to commit to this Guru".

I asked him a question out of inquisitiveness. "What were you doing closing your eyes?"

"Nothing", he said. "I was doing nothing".

"What do you mean by nothing?"

"My son, I was just there. I was not doing anything. I was silent."

"Which means you should be either thinking something or dreaming about days to come"?

"No dear. When I am in silence neither I think nor dream. I am just there."

"What do you get by doing that?"

"Answers, my son", he said, "I get answers. I feel a sense of connection. I get associated with everything and everything gets associated with me. I become one with all."

"Then?" I asked curiously.

"I get what I seek—a direction".

"Who will give you what you need?"

"No one my son. No one will give me what I want. But I get connected to the path which guides me to the coincidences and opportunities on my journey. I cannot measure exactly what I get. But I accept what I get and respect the choices I make on that divine path of guidance".

"Actually, I am really not sure about how much I followed. But my father and granny had told me similar things about coincidences in life".

"It's time for your first task Shikar", said the Guru, "I want you to execute it very sincerely".

"Do I have to do some tasks?"

"You committed", the Guru said.

"Bring it on", I said," I am known to execute tasks with perfection at my office".

The Guru smiled and said, "I want you to sit here in the same way as I did and be silent with your eyes closed for the next 15 minutes".

"What would I do sitting silently? I can't. I am not a monk like you to just be doing nothing."

"Neither am I, my son. I am not a monk too. Can you get into the task? We have many tasks to be accomplished over these three days."

I sat down on the rock he pointed to and closed my eyes. I tried to sit erect as he corrected my posture. Closing my eyes, I tried to focus on silence. It was not easy. Though I was not uttering a word, there was tremendous turbulence in my mind. My mind was full of thoughts. Who is this man? What is he trying to do with me? What am I doing here? Will Pundit be back on Wednesday? My boss . . . What are Simone and Aarav doing?"

Opening my eyes, I told the Guru, "I am not able to focus on being silent. I am not able to stop thinking. How can anyone do that? There are numerous things flashing in my mind."

"Son, I will tell you what the basic problem is. In fact there are two of them. First, you are trying to focus on silence. Never do that. In silence there is peace. Where peace is, there is neither force nor an effort to do something. It is not wrong to get thoughts. Just let them come and go. Just do not try to stick on to them. Be an observer."

"And the second one?" I asked curiously.

"Do it for YOU. Not because I asked you to do", said the Guru.

I closed my eyes again. Most of the thoughts repeated. But this time, I just tried to observe them. They passed and I was just there not doing anything with them. After some more time, my thoughts slowed down. The gap between the thoughts started to widen and there I found the access to silence. It was a fabulous feeling. I was feeling a sense of joy, peace and stability that the silence had to offer. My thoughts almost disappeared at one stage. Rarely one of those appeared and then dissolved into the power of stillness and silence that I was experiencing.

I stayed there. Just with me and myself. Nothing seemed more important than that moment. I forgot everything and did not think of anything ahead. Neither past nor future had any influence on my state of being. I was filled with the joy of presence. Just presence and nothing else. I was out of the bonds of time and space. I was just there.

"My son", I heard the soft voice. "Awaken", called the Guru, who brought me out of that world of stillness.

"I think I have awakened", I said, referring the deeper meaning of what I experienced. "Thank you so much", I said.

"Why do you thank me, Shikar?"

"I felt something, which I never experienced till now in my entire life. You made it possible", I said.

"You made it possible by yourself, my son", he said with his trademark smile on his face.

"I want to do this every day. It's a great feeling. It's like a rebirth."

"I am happy that you want to experience it every day. Now, that you learnt it, it is possible. But it is not sufficient."

"What else do you expect me to do?" I asked anxiously.

"Know who you are, my son."

"What do you mean by knowing who I am. I am Shikar; working in a multinational company, earning a decent salary for my age and experience. A loving husband and a good father. I think I know what I am, what my likes and dislikes are and where I am heading in my life."

"That's not sufficient my son. They are the roles you are playing. They are the roles you have adopted yourself to. They are not YOU."

"Then what are they. Or, who am I?"

"You will get the answer in that state of just being. The state of silence and stillness. You will get the answer. Again, please remember. Don't try hard. Just be. You will get the answer. Just observe."

I was not able to believe what the Guru told me. Whatever it was, I was blown away by the experience of stillness. May be what he told about knowing myself also had something exciting. I wanted to give a try.

"Shikar, do you know what the time now is?"

I answered that it should be close to 8 AM. I spent an hour and a half talking to him and I would have spent a 15 min in the task. So I expected an estimate of 2 hrs from the time I reached that place.

"It is 11 AM now", he answered with a gentle smile. I was dumb struck. I could not imagine that I spent so much of my time there. How did the time pass so fast?

"How did the time go so fast? Where did we spend the time?"

"In the task my son, you were in the state of silence for three and a half hours"

I could not believe what he was saying. I asked him why did I spend so much time in the task and I did not even know. What was I doing? Did I sleep? But I was sure I did not. I was able to feel that I was in a much more awakened state that I normally be. I was feeling everything. But what exactly happened? I asked the Guru.

"The first thing that I want you to get out of is the illusion of time. I want you to get liberated from the bond of time. There is nothing called time. We have created it and we are being ruled by it now. The primary thing that any seeker of peace and real calling needs to do is to be liberated and extremely present in the moment. Now, to answer your question, you were actually doing nothing. You had reached your essential state of purity and stability. You were extremely present in every moment. You entered the zone of timelessness. You were in a state of peaceful and awakened consciousness."

But I felt that I took a lot of time to reach that state of pure and awakened consciousness. I questioned the same.

"Shikar, the state of stillness and the time to reach that state are both determined by three important factors."

"Which are . . . ?" I asked eagerly.

"The first one is purity of our thoughts, words and actions. As long as there is a harmony of love and purity in your thoughts, words and actions, your soul will be in sync with pure consciousness and will lead you to the state of stillness. It is not sufficient if you execute actions projecting greatness, while the inner state of mind is exactly thinking the opposite. It is not correct to speak softly whereas the thoughts behind are very harsh. This state of being never takes you to the state of still and conscious awakening. Usually, the thoughts that we have are mostly about the past or the future. For a state of stillness, we need to eliminate these unwanted thoughts on which we do not exercise any control and free the mind to be in the divinity of presence."

"The second principle is consumption of right food. When you nourish your body with the right food, it brings you a peaceful mind. This kind of food is known as satvic food in Sanskrit. Food that we take has a great impact on the state of your mind. Food which is as close to the natural state as possible, keeps your mind balanced."

"Now the third principle; It is the way you take care of your physical body, the residence of your soul. We ignore the body taking it for granted. But it's a great sin. We go to the temple where we worship God. For me, the universal soul is God. It has no space and time and is everywhere and nowhere at the same time. But we, the individual souls who are a fragment of the universal soul are provided with the temple which is our body. We should keep our bodies clean and healthy and respect them, the way we do with any place for worshipping God".

The three principles that the Guru taught made perfect sense. I decided that I implement them with immediate effect. The Guru asked me to repeat the task and this time find the answers to the life's basic questions.

"What are the basic questions of life?"

- What is my Dharma?
- What is that the universal soul seeks from me?

- Why am I created?
- Who am I?

These were few questions that the Guru prompted. I registered them by taking a deep breath and reiterating them in my mind silently.

Closing my eyes, I went into silence again. This time it was easier to get into silence compared to the earlier trials. Each question started popping up one by one and I waited effortlessly for the answers. If I had magical powers that allowed me to do whatever I wanted to do what is that I would do? Usually, when we ask some questions to ourselves, they carry a limitation, which is in form of doubt and fear. But in this state, the questions did not have any limit. If I have to move the world what is that I would do?

Many questions passed through the silence. As the rule stated, I just observed them. Finally the most basic, simple, immensely sensible, yet tremendously powerful question knocked the silence. I felt massive power, extreme courage, immense bliss and joy. I felt that I ruled the world and the world listened to me. If I found answer for that simple question, I would do justice to this momentary projection of the universal soul through this lifetime. The question was-

WHAT I REALLY WANT TO DO in THE WAY THAT I WANT TO DO, ANYTIME and EVERYTIME?

I waited for the answer. I can live life as stated above only when I do what I love to do; I do what I am extremely interested in and do it effortlessly. In that state of silence, I never set any boundaries on my thoughts that were passing through. There was no evaluation process for the answers that would flow. There was no process of acceptance or rejection. It was just to seek and observe. I waited for the answer in that state.

My childhood events started flashing in my mind. We had a music school just 100 steps away from my home. I was about ten years old. My mom asked me to join the music class; I told her that I just wanted to play with my friends. After school, I did not waste any time. Quickly we completed our homework, even while having our shoes on, sitting in the balcony of my house. Then it was time to play. My house was filled with trophies, which I won for singing what my dad wrote. I did not join the music school not because I did not like to. I feared I would lose my friends. I loved music. I grew up seeing concerts in our small colony, singing my dad's songs, listening and watching Michael Jackson's albums. I loved the way he created music. I would even miss my play if there was Michael's show broadcasted on television. I always wanted to hold a guitar and sing. I sang alone. I did not need audience. When I had audience I had a lot to offer them, which I did seamlessly. I never thought of anything when I was singing. I just was in a similar state of bliss that I experienced in the silence. Though I did not learn music in a school, I was capable of singing anything effortlessly. I loved any kind of music.

I was a good student too. I stood either first or second in the class. My parents were normal. They loved me so much as any parents would. They had the traditional mindset of School, College, Job and retirement. I also believed that it was life. If I get a job in a big company, my life would be settled. This was what I always thought of life.

My dad wrote poems when I was very young; may be less than 6 years old. He had a book of poems. That was the only book he wrote. Mom used to give me one of those poems and I practiced them for singing competitions. He stopped writing once he grew up the ladder in his office. I realized now that he started spending lesser time with me because he did not have enough. He did not even have time for his passion of writing. Those days I did not realize this. I spent a lot of time with mom.

My dad worked very hard and came very late from office every day. He used to be silent after he was back from office and was always thinking of some problems at work. As a routine, he had to give a call to his boss at 8 PM to report the number of tons of limestone that were shipped for production of cement. That call decided how he spent the rest of the day before we slept; leave alone spending time, it decided if he would have a peaceful sleep that night. It hurt me a lot. I did not know how much he was hurt. He could neither live his dream nor live a happy life with his family. One thing that he did was, he played a great role as a father. He secured our future. I remember him saying me that once he gets retired, he would write poems, teach Mathematics to school students and geology to Miners. But . . . his life ended even before it actually started.

I loved his poems. He was very happy when he wrote. He was the happiest when he shared his poems with us. I remember the pride of that great poet when he offered his work to others. He had a great sense of joy seeing his poems sung by children. I think the only thing I could give him was a part of that joy he experienced when his son sang his poems and won accolades.

Music!!

Music was my dream. Huge Stream of pleasure and happiness rushed into my heart as I could see the answer that flashed through the glimpses of my childhood. I felt that dad spoke to me knocking at my soul's door reminding me my purpose. That's why they say that the soul never goes anywhere. It always finds a place to express itself. I opened my eyes.

"Music is my dream. I am here to sing and create wonderful Music."

It was the most precious moment of my life; when I shared my dream with the Guru. I was full of pride.

"I am very happy for you as you have realized your dream, my son. Remember what you have learnt. Life has everything in abundance to offer you, as long as you do not struggle to get it. Be effortless; path will show up. Follow the path. Live your dream. My son, go ahead and live your dream".

"But Guru . . . I discovered what is my dream. It makes me very happy. But how do I realize it?"

"What is stopping you my son? As you discovered your dream, why don't you go and just live it?"

"Guru, I don't know what is stopping me. There is a sense of fear, when I think that I should work on my dream".

I realized what stopped my father. This sense of fear stopped him. As long as we are doing what we are doing, and be in the routine accepted by all, we feel everything is fine. As we try to disturb the routine, we feel that sense of fear which pulls us out of the comfortable and assumed state of happiness.

"Guru, I am really scared of this thought of pursuing my dream. I need a big help from you. Please make me understand the reason for this fear and help me find the path of happiness."

"I do not know the answer", said the Guru.

"From the time I met you, you have told me many things about myself. You helped me identify my dream. You helped me fill my mind with clarity. So I am sure you know how to help me with this. Please tell me."

"The only person who can answer your question is YOU. No one can help you find answer for your questions. Being a good friend of yours, what I can do is to help you discover something which you already know. That is how any learning does happen, my son. All the concepts that I taught you till now are what you already knew. Whenever you hear something, your mind selectively picks details from the collective pool of your experiences stored in your soul and provides the required information. That is what knowledge is. To help you out in finding answer from yourself, I can teach you something. However, execution is left to you."

"Please go on", I said fervently waiting for him to proceed.

"You have to practice SVADHYAYA", said the Guru.

"What does it mean? I fairly remember that my granny used this word, while she was talking to my dad. Can you help me with the meaning of this word?"

"Svadhyaya is a word in the ancient language Sanskrit originated in India. "Sva", means "self" and "Adhyaya" means "study". So it is the study of the self. This is considered as a powerful practice and is the path to attain eternal peace and enlightenment. As you study yourself and learn from your life, you will be a teacher and student simultaneously. As you practice this technique every day, you learn and master the subject of universal consciousness, which is nothing but the path to realization of GOD. You become one with the Universe.

Okay now, it's time to execute the learning. Close your eyes and start the study of self. Please remember, this should be an effortless practice. Place the intention in silence and just wait for the answers."

I was excited and tensed at the same time. I was not sure if I would really find the reason for my fear to live my dream. However, as the earlier trials, I decided to believe in this one too and started the task.

I closed my eyes and focused on my breath, as it was one of the techniques which the Guru taught me to get into silence. It worked. I was in a state of silence. I placed the intention of living my dream. There was a slight discomfort as before. I decided to stick on and wait for the answers. I started observing the flash of images which are the clues. Answers started coming . . . one by one.

Simone and I fell in love and got married 6 years ago. We worked in the same firm where we got close to each other. I liked her because she was independent, sensible and a very sweet girl. She liked me because I lived the way I wanted and was full of values which were very significant part of me. She loves me a lot and supports me in whatever effort I take. We built a small house and Aarav entered our lives 4 years back. We are a happy family with a solid plan for future. We decided to save 20% of my income for Aarav's education and his future. I was repaying the bank for the loan on my house. I get a good pay to lead a comfortable life. Simone earned a small amount as she shifted her profession to teaching children from being software professional. She had taken a break when Aarav was born. She is working just to keep herself occupied and also she loved being with kids.

I that state of silence, I was observing myself as if someone else was observing me.

Now, that was my life. It was so organized. And that's was an obstacle too. Actually, there was more than one obstacle that I could retrieve out of what I just saw. I was living a comfortable life. So, the fear that popped up when I started to think about living my dream was due to the disturbance in this organized and comfortable status quo.

Many questions flashed one after the other as I saw my own life like a movie. Will Simone like the idea of living my dream? How will I repay my loan if I quit my job? What about the financial security for my family? What will happen to Aarav's future? Finally, what if this whole stuff of living my dream does not work at all?

I opened my eyes. I explained the Guru, whatever I saw.

"So many obstacles Guru. That's what I could find as answers for the fear of living my dream. Obstacles of love, commitment and comfort. The only obstacle which I believe, can be removed is of Simone's support. I am sure that she would support me. She loves me so much. But what about the rest? With so many obstacles, how can anyone live their dream?"

The Guru smiled again. I could read his smile. He was going teach some new concept. I waited eagerly. The Guru shared a story.

"There was a small boy in a village. His father was a farmer. He would go to the farm every day and work very hard. He had a bullock cart. He would travel everywhere in that bullock cart. One day the boy wanted to go to the farm with his father and the father agreed to take him along. The boy was very happy. Next morning, he got up early and was ready to go with his father. He was full of pride as he sat next to his father who was riding the bullock cart. As their farm was nearer to the city, there were many vehicles in the route through which they travelled. The father observed something. Whenever a vehicle passed, though the boy did not utter a word, he held his father tightly. He was getting scared. The father asked his son why he was getting scared when vehicles passed by. The little boy admitted that he was scared because he felt their bullock cart would be hit by the vehicles and they would get hurt. The father smiled and said, "Son, remember 2 things in life. First, never look at the obstacles on your way as bad ones. Every obstacle has something to offer. If there was never a vehicle on the road that I travelled, I would never know how to navigate. The second important thing to learn from the obstacles is that they help us think all the possibilities of finding a way out and make us strong and capable to lead our life."

The boy then started looking at the gap whenever a vehicle came, through which his father was easily moving forward and finally reached their destination."

I understood the essence of what the Guru wanted to explain.

The Guru continued, "Shikar, in the story that I mentioned, the boy's father uses a whip to control the bull. The father in the story is like our soul, the whip is the mind and the bull is our body. The soul triggers the mind which in turn commands the body. So, it is very important to connect the soul which leads us to possibilities."

"What is soul? And where is it?" I asked as I was confused with what is the difference between these two commonly used words-mind and soul.

"I will provide you the answer for this question on the last day of our meeting", the Guru said. "My son, the essence is that you focus on the possibilities that life offers you rather than the obstacles."

"Let us meet tomorrow. You can go back to your hotel for today. Remember to be here on time tomorrow morning."

I was happy that the first day of our meeting ended. But at the same time I started liking the Guru very much for what he had done to me. I actually started to realize that I have started to live again. I was really not much worried about who the Guru was. Though I was curious to know the person who knew almost everything about me, I decided to wait till the third day.

"I can stay for little more time if you want me to", I said.

"No, my son. The lesson for today is over. YOU DISCOVERED YOURSELF. Please go now as it is getting late and is about to get dark. Kindly remember whatever I taught today and follow each concept that I taught you religiously. Let us meet tomorrow".

"Are you not scared to stay here alone?" I asked looking around the place where we were, near to his hut, in that mountain range.

"Good night", smiled the Guru.

He did not answer that question. In fact, he had not answered many of my questions. I decided that I would ask those questions on the Day 3. On my way back, all the concepts that the Guru taught me flashed in my mind. I was happy that Mr. Pundit was not in station. I could learn much more from the Guru. The only thing that I was missing was my family.

I reached the hotel. It was 7 PM. I did not have anything since 6AM the morning. I never realized that I was hungry till I reached the hotel. I was so involved in the conversation that I never thought of food. One more pleasant feature about that place was the climate was always cool and never hinted me about time. Deciding to have an early dinner, I went to the restaurant at the hotel. I remembered what the Guru spoke about satvic food, which meant a good light vegetarian food closer to its natural state. I had a good salad and very light food. I enjoyed the food by eating in a state of complete consciousness. I was a good feeling. I had some homework which I carried with me after the meeting with Guru. As I walked to my room I could hear the chorus of frogs and other insects. Truly I started feeling more present and conscious. I was feeling that every other creature is a part of me and I had a sense of connection with them. I decided to sit for some time and then go to the room. I had to go to bed early so that I could wake up early and meet the Guru on time, the next day.

What a day it was! I learnt few of life's beautiful and most important concepts. I did not want to forget those amazing concepts. Immediately I walked to my room and picked a pen and a journal. My father told me that if you want to remember something, write it down so that you can refer to it whenever you want.

I came out of the room and sat on a bench under a small lamp. It was very pleasant. I could not hear anything other than the sound of insects and frogs. I have not experienced this for more than a decade. Father took me to granny's village for my vacation. It was very silent and calm there. But, my heart never asked for that serenity. In fact I did not realize that there was so much joy in silence, in that small age.

I wrote few affirmations in my journal.

- I would always have pure and positive thoughts, which would help me bring purity to my words and actions.
- I would respect my body and take satvic food.
- I would practice Svadhyaya every day to study and monitor my state of being and my progress towards my purpose.
- Having discovered my Dharma (Purpose) of life, I would work on all the possibilities to fulfill the same.

As I wrote my last affirmation, I remembered the task which I had to complete. I started thinking of all the possibilities that would help me fulfill my dharma. I thought that the wise way to do it is to identify all possibilities to remove my obstacles.

I wanted to pursue music as my career. When I am involved in music, I was timeless.

I listed down the obstacles and also all the possibilities to overcome them.

I built a small house in my place. I had the mortgage I was paying every month. It consumed about 25% of my income. If I had an unexpected spend in any particular month, I would miss one of the payments, which would result in a penalty and increased interest. I was wondering how I would manage that 25% of my income when I completely come out of a regular pay. Now, that was the obstacle number one.

To implement the learning of the day, I went into silence placing the intention of identifying all possibilities to manage loan repayment which was due for next 15 years. Slowly, ideas started flowing in. I started listing them down. There were many ideas. I did not ignore even one of them. I respected each and every possibility and listed them down. They were so varied and dissimilar from what I would think of in a normal state, for example, sitting in my office cabin. I numbered them and there were 28 of them. I had no clue about what I could do to my loan just an hour before. Now I have got 28 possible ways to do it.

I started to go through the list of ideas. Though I would not want to list all of those, I will let you know the most interesting one which was really challenging and gave me a high when I thought of. I decided to clear off all the loans, including my house, car and other furnishings in next 2 years against 14 years. Now, this was the most challenging idea. I did not have any clue on how I would do that. But I placed it strong in my head and decided that it was a major step towards my dream. I underlined that idea.

I could link and use most of the other ideas to achieve this one. Few were like changing my job, looking for a better job for Simone, pooling all the money and making short term investments, deciding to sell few properties, moving to a smaller house which would still be comfortable for a small family like ours, prepare a proper monthly budget and cut-down the spend that was not required, borrow money from few best friends to whom I can return as interest free installments and many more ideas. When I linked all the income out of these ideas to this short term goal, I found that it was very much achievable. Wow! It was an amazing feeling to know that I can overcome the most important obstacle in the next 2 years.

Now I was getting clearer on the process. I realized that, what we want to achieve, can be achieved only if we focus on that intention and spend sufficient time on achieving it.

As I thought of time, I understood that this was the second major obstacle. I wanted time to work on my craft. I needed a lot of practice to master my singing and learn the musical instruments. I work for 10 hours a day at office. Travel to office consumed another 2 hours. I listed the activities and time spent by me every day including sleep. I had nothing left. In fact the 24 hours of each day were not sufficient. Now that was a great obstacle to work on.

Minimum 2 hours every day had to be squeezed out for practice. Again I listed all the possibilities where I can buy some time out, getting into the state of silence. Many ideas started flowing once again. Changing job nearer to where I was living or shifting closer to where I was working. This would save me 2 hours. Also, I could think of a job where I can work for 8 hours and earn a better pay. I knew I was very much capable of working faster, smarter and better. I was just comfortable in the current job as I did not think of a day that would trigger my inner fire.

As I was thinking of possibilities, I was able to link the possibilities of both obstacles; money and time. I can find a job which paid higher and was also near to where I live. This way I can manage both the requirements. Also, as I had to attend a music class to learn from a good musician, the search became more refined. I had to be in a place where

I am closer to both my music class and better paying job. Further refined was the idea of looking for a higher pay job for Simone nearby the new location. Finally, find a good school for Aarav in that location.

There I was ready with my desirable criteria checklist. It was ultra-clear, sure shot way to overcome my obstacles of money and time, work on my craft and be ready to fly in next 2 years. I started fantasizing about the future, which had no option than to happen for me. It was an awesome state. Wow! I have a vision in my life.

My phone started ringing. Simone called. I picked up and said, "I love you honey. I just realized why I was born".

"What are you saying? Are you OK? Love you so much. Tell me what happened?" Simone said. She was wondering why I was speaking something very strange. I told her that our life is going to change forever. I realized that happiness is the goal of life and it can be achieved only through constant work on one's Dharma. I told her about my meeting with the Guru, who was teaching me few simple yet amazing concepts of life. She sensed the peaceful and positive vibrations I generated. Simone was very happy about the change I was experiencing. She told me that it was 10 PM and urged me to get proper sleep, so that I can meet the Guru at the right time. Simone was more excited and eager to hear complete story of my meeting with Guru, on my return.

Hectic work schedule had taken a toll over my sleeping habits. I reached home at 10 PM, slept at 12 or 1 AM and got up at 7 AM every day. Work, an hour of chat with Simone and sleep; this was my schedule. I spent some time with Aarav in the mornings helping him get ready for school.

Now, I decided this was not going to be my schedule anymore. I will create my day and schedule my work and no one else would have a say on that. Sense of victory over myself astonished me. What a guy Guru was! He created such an impact in just one day to my entire life. I fixed the alarm at 4:30 AM and fell asleep.

Day 2:
THE PROPHECY OF DHARMA

I was up and ready by 5 AM. Walking towards the mountain, I was thinking about the great impact of learning I had; and I also was anxious about what the Guru was going to teach on the second day. I reached the place by 5:30 AM. As I waited for him, I started wondering again; who is the guy who knows so much about me? Is he a magician who can read people? Who is he? Anyways I was more interested in what I had to learn than think of this mysterious person.

"I told you not to think of who I am," I heard the Guru's voice.

"I hope Simone was happy about the change you are undergoing here on these hills. She is waiting to hear from you the entire story of your transformation."

"How do you know what happens with me? Can you do this with everyone or only your powers are specific to me?"

"You will know it by the end of our meeting tomorrow my son," he said.

"Did you do the homework? Did you find ways to overcome your obstacles?"

"Yes", I said in an exuberant tone, "I used the concepts I learned from you and was able to identify all the possibilities to resolve the obstacles on my way to achieve my dream".

"I am very glad I have realized that I have a dream and also a path to achieve it. It was one of the happiest moments I had in the recent years. Silence and Svadhyaya were two great tools that did wonders. I noted down every possibility of realizing my dream. Also, I started to purify my thoughts, words and deeds by being ultra-conscious in each and every thing I do. Actually being pure, helped me be in silence and I also felt more conscious and present most of the time. Most of the thoughts I had earlier were based on assumptions. Being pure and silent helped me to be my true self. Simone was really happy as she felt my positive vibrations. Thank you so much for yesterday. I hope even you could feel my positive energy. Now, I am very confident to reach my destiny defined by my dream and created by myself."

The Guru listened quietly. There was no change in his expression as I expressed my happiness. I paused for a while and asked him, "Are you not happy about the change you brought in me? You have done an incomparable job which I never dreamt of. You paved a new path for me. Why are you so silent now and not saying anything?"

"Shikar, please remember one thing. I want you to understand that you have achieved a great milestone by realizing what you want to express. The point is that it is still in you, waiting to be expressed. Many people fail at this point of their journey. They discover what they are meant to be. They do not start working on it. They would remember their dream for few days or months. Then gradually the normalcy takes over and they are back into the conformed process of being. The conformity they choose is to be in the acceptance of society and not to self. They would never take even the first step towards their expected expression of soul.

There are few more people, who dare to take the first step. They start with a lot of enthusiasm. They start as if nothing can stop them. Then they face the world with this enthusiasm. On their way, life starts teaching them by experiences. As soon as an unfavorable situation is presented by life, they immediately plunge back to normalcy. They associate that situation with negativity instead of treating it as an opportunity presented by life to groom them. Every situation is an experience. Experience can neither be bad nor good. It is just an experience. We make it good or bad based on what we believe. That belief in turn is an accumulation of the accepted criteria in the society in which we are born and brought up.

Then there is the third category of people who are not more than 1% of the people in this world who follow their dream with continued focus. They refine their path constantly, learning out of experiences and working hard with dedication to achieve their dreams. They are not bothered about what the rest of the world thinks. They are not in the trap of conformance standards set by the society. They follow their calling with joy and pride. They are the people with the highest self-esteem. They are passionate about their dream and constantly ensure that they are on the path which is in sync with what the universal soul wanted from them.

My son, I want you to be in this category. I know that you are extremely happy about finding your calling. But remember that just finding is not receiving. You have to put all your effort to reach there. Svadhyaya practice, I taught you, not just for identification of your dream; it is a practice that you do every day to continuously study your progress and remove the obstacles, till you reach your dream. I want you to realize that happiness is a state of mind. As long as it is based on your set of beliefs as a reference, it is just momentary. The day your reference changes to yourself and not your beliefs based on the acceptance standards of the society, happiness becomes eternal and you will be at peace and joy irrespective of what happens outside you.

Son, now please tell me what is that you realized yesterday night at the hotel. I would like to know how clear you are about your dream. I hope that you have aligned your dharma to your dream. Please tell me now."

I listened very carefully to whatever the Guru told me. I started to elaborate on what I saw in silence at the hotel.

"Music is my passion and I would be making a career out of it. I am very clear on this and I have prepared a real solid plan ready for execution. Nothing can stop the plan from working. I am going to clear off all my loans in the next 2 years and then quit my job. Then I will take a loan and open an audio recording studio. I will hire some people and start creating albums. We will sell the album and then make money out of it. That's the plan. I have listed all the possibilities that will make this plan work. What do you think about it Guru?"

"That is really good to hear my son. But can you tell me how big your dream is?"

"What do you mean by how big?"

"What is that you want to achieve on your path and where is that you would want to reach?"

"I do not know. I never thought of it. I just wanted to start working on my dream. I never had an image in my mind as to how far I should reach. Is it a sort of goal or something that you are trying to mention? I am sorry but I do not have any at the moment. Is it a problem not to have a goal in mind as we start working on our dreams?"

"Yes it is very important. Why don't you create one now? Just be silent and then try to pen your goal in your mind. Close your eyes."

"How big is your dream? Why don't you see in the state of silence, the size of your dream?"

I closed my eyes and I started to visualize what I can be in what I have discovered as my dream. I thought of arriving at a measure so that I can express it in a specific number to the Guru. I am working now in a job that pays me a handsome amount of money. With that pay, what I am able to do is to take care of my family, go for 2 vacations a year and provide a decent education for my son. If I quit, then I should be able to take care of myself and family the same way as I did when I was in a job. So, if I earn out of my dream, what I am earning now by doing a job; that would be a good goal and size of my dream.

I opened my eyes.

"Out of my dream, which is to make a career in music on my own, I would want to earn 60,000 rupees per month, which I am earning now, out of my job. This would allow me to lead a good life. So that is the size of my dream". As I said this to the Guru there was a sense of pride in me. I felt very happy that I could put a number against my dream. Eagerly I waited for the Guru's approval on my finding.

The Guru gave his signature smile.

"What . . . am I not right in fixing a goal? I thought it is a great one. I was excited as I got a measure to my goal. I thought it was perfect."

"I am happy about the direction of your thinking, which is, to put a measure against your dream. But there are 2 fundamental errors in your thinking".

"What are they?"

"The first one is to put money as a measure to realizing your dream. Money is always the resultant of your dream. You should be driven by your dream and not the money you get out of it. Your dream is a beautiful one. You are going to make people happy by following your dream. As you realize your dream, you will become more and more fulfilled and you create a positive impact on people's lives as you move ahead on the path. As you move past various milestones on your path, the universe grants you so much in return and one of them can be money. Money is one of the numerous results on your road to destiny or Dharma.

Define your goal in terms of what your Dharma has to deliver in this universe of countless opportunities and infinite possibilities. Think of the impact that you are supposed to create on the universe, so that in return you will make the world a better place than it was.

Think of how much you can give; how many lives you can touch and how much positive change you bring in this world. How many people can you make happy today? How many people can you help today, in realizing their dreams? Everyone in this world needs one thing, which they are not consciously aware"

"What is that?" I asked eagerly.

"Happiness!

Everyone wants to be happy. Happiness is the ultimate goal of each and every human being in this world. Happiness is the ultimate result they expect out of whatever they do. Take an example of you. You want to realize your dream of making a career out of music. What does it bring you? What happens to you when you are listening to music or playing music?"

The answer was obvious. I would feel extremely happy. I would forget myself while I am practicing. I would be in a place where I feel I am in a beautiful world of my own.

"So, my son, the first mistake is to associate your dream with money."

I was clear on what Guru explained. Also it made a lot of sense. The bigger the dream, the greater the impact and the greater the drive to fulfill.

"I am very clear on what you said and in fact it was an eye opener for me. Usually money drives people for some time, but over a period of time that does not really bring out the best in you."

"Most of the people who are not in the conventional breed of the approved flow, which is *study—job—retirement— end of life* would start working on their dream. Eventually they would get caught up in the web of money which is given the most important place by the conventional breed and end up nowhere on their journey towards destiny. They get back to the normal accepted standards of living, defined by society and move on in life. Or they get depressed and lead an unhappy life for the rest of their presence on this earth. Those who return to the conventional breed would remember their dream once in a while, for some time and feel that they did a mistake, and learnt a lot out of that experience of failure. They also spoil few others in their circle of influence and feel proud about it thinking that they are doing the right thing by giving that piece of advice to that potential few, or else, they would have ended up with a miserable life. But when the final knock on the door arrives, they realize that they did not live. They realize that, the small hiccup on their journey which they could not use as learning, the fear that cropped up which did not allow trying another possibility, the group of so called advisory board who always ensured that you are on the approved path—all were just what they created themselves. No one else . . .

Money is just a means of transaction. It can never be a measure of you and your dream"

That brought a much better clarity. Images of many people who experienced failure, the advisory board as the Guru called were readily available in me and flashed in no time as he was speaking the truth of the mind-ruled world.

I remembered something. "You said I made two mistakes. I understand the first one, which the measure of my dream. It's ultra-clear now. What is the second one?"

"It's the size of your dream my son. As you change your measure, you will automatically change the size of your dream. I want you to redefine the measure of your dream, so that I can help you with the size."

I recollected what the Guru said while explaining the mistake of the measure of my dream. Now, I started thinking on the impact that my dream can create. Music makes people happy and connected to the divine. It supports the unity of individual soul and the universal soul. As a result of which one would feel lighter, peaceful, and yes . . . happy.

I want to make as many people happy as possible. So, that's the measure. The number of people I can reach out to. How can I reach a number of people? Of course by doing music shows. I wanted to reach all the people in my town and do shows in all the auditoriums of my town.

As I thought this, I was inspired so much. I was visualizing myself doing shows in all the auditoriums of my city. I would be famous and also I would touch thousands of people in the process. I was also little scared. I told the Guru what I thought.

"Guru, I have defined the size of my dream now. I would touch all the people in my town, which would be a sizeable number. I would be famous in my town and do shows in all the auditoriums which would cover all the areas of my town. I can make my entire town happier than they were. In the process, as you said, I would be earning a good amount of money as a result. I think the change of measure of my dream has helped me expand the size to a significant extent. However, I am feeling little scared as I have few doubts in achieving this big goal. What do you think? Is this too big? Is it achievable?"

The Guru was quiet for a while. I felt he was thinking something very deeply about what I just said.

"Hmmm . . . how can you judge something as a possibility or not even without having experienced it?" he asked.

I was not so clear on the question. So I asked him to deliberate.

"We have standards set in our minds due to our experience and exposure. From our childhood we would have faced many struggles and had many good experiences which would have taught their share to us. Each and every person whom we met for a short time or as long as many years, would have spoken many things to us on their views of good and bad about various aspects of life. Now, all these experiences either good or bad would frame an idea and standard for everything in our mind. So these ideas and standards become the reference points. Whenever we have to decide something, we check with the standards set in mind. Then the best decision would be out of the best in the range of standards available. Which means—we try to reach the best of what is in our mind, but not the real best.

In fact there is nothing called the real best. It is not known to anyone. That's why it is said that there are unlimited possibilities. Whatever is known as best is not the actual best in reality. It is only in the mind. As we work towards our goals, thinking of possibilities that are limited by the already set standards in our mind, we usually set goals which are small.

In actual, YOU CAN CONQUER THE WORLD."

That statement struck the right chord in me. What an amazing statement, the Guru made. Yes, it's true. There are people who literally conquered the world. Without a vision that's so huge, how could that be possible? How could Alexander do it? How could people like Mahatma Gandhi do it? How could Henry Ford do it? They had their dreams which were thought to be unreal and criticized by many when they started off. But they proved to the world that they have the capability to conquer anything. However, it was the powerful vision that these people had. Their dream was bigger than the then known reality and never had any boundaries. They dared to think beyond. Once they thought, it formed their vision—a measurable vision. They saw it happening in their mind. They experienced it before it happened in reality. They set a new standard in their mind. That's how they redefined the possibility. They conquered the world of their dreams.

I was filled with immense poise. I decided that I would have a goal that would be beyond the world of possibilities. As the Guru said, I would set an amazingly great standard in my mind and work towards it. I asked the Guru, "What about the obstacles? Did they not have any obstacles on their way? How could they deal with those obstacles?"

The Guru said, "The great people whom I mentioned just now are those whose stories are heard by all of us. We all heard of the obstacles they had. But it's not the obstacles that guided them. It was their vision which drove them to reach those heights. They were not known as great people before they reached their goals. They became famous mostly after they achieved them or while they were on their path with utmost commitment to their vision. They were ordinary people before they saw their vision clearly in their mind. They never thought of any obstacle. In fact they were bold and fearless. Nothing else mattered other than the picture of their vision painted in their minds.

Remember one thing. What you see in your mind is what you will get. Remember the bullock cart story. As long as you see the obstacles, you will not be able to move past them and get to encounter more of them in your life. Those great people saw only what they wanted to achieve and they never focused on obstacles. So they got to see more of opportunities than the obstacles on their journey. What they had was the courage to move forward and overcome those obstacles. Also they learnt a lot from those experiences.

So tremendous COURAGE to dream and tread on your path is the most important feature that anyone who wants to live rather than just exist, should possess. My son . . . be fearless. Have the courage to dream and see your biggest vision. Don't allow the old conditioning and standards to influence you. You have no restrictions other than the ones laid by yourself. You are entitled to dream and receive whatever you wish for with clarity, belief, sincerity, commitment and courage. Just follow this . . .

The world will work for you."

I felt an incredible positive energy rushing in and filling me up with tons of confidence. I suddenly felt that I had no bounds. I felt that I can do anything I wanted. I can choose whatever I wanted, than follow what I am expected to, by anyone in this society.

My goal of doing shows in all the auditoriums of my town seemed like a much smaller one. My capability supported by the universal force would move the world. Why should I limit my vision? Now there is nothing that could stop me. I wanted to revisit my dream with more clarity and nail it down. I just thought for a while—how many lives can I impact with my field of music? Everyone in this world. Has anyone ever made it so big in this field? Of course yes . . . My idol—Michael Jackson. Yes . . . he made it. He created something that moved the world. His music was awesome. People cried happy tears listening to it. He moved their souls. He made the world happy.

"I want to be the next Michael Jackson. I want to be just like him—the king of pop. I like his music. I would do a similar music like that of Jackson. That would help me in realizing my dream which is now larger than everything and beyond imagination. Now, what do you think? This goal is really big and is inspiring me. Whatever are the obstacles on my way, I would overcome them being fearless", I stated with confidence reaching its peak.

"Shikar, it's nice to hear what you just said. I am happy about it. I would like to tell you a story which I heard long back. This might help you.

Once upon a time, in a far off town, there were two friends who knew each other from their childhood. Their names were Athil and Saif. Athil was very good at studies. He always secured a good rank in his class. Athil's father worked in a big factory. So Athil was from a very well-to-do family. He had everything he wanted.

On the other hand, Saif was not much into studies. He was a boy with good values. He was taught life lessons by his father. As his father was working for daily wages, he

Vishnu Sharma

could not get proper education. His father learnt what life had to teach him and he imparted his learning to his only son.

Both the boys grew up. They completed their education. Athil came out with flying colors as a topper in the class. Saif completed as an average student. Athil got a job in his father's factory. Saif could not get any job. He was at home, searching for a job. His father was worried. One day Saif's uncle visited their town on his way for a business trip. He took shelter in Saif's house for 2 days.

Khaja Khan was Saif's uncle. He was a diamond merchant. He made good money. Saif's parents tried to be a good host to whatever extent possible. Khaja Khan was a person who had seen the world. He could sense that his sister's family is in trouble. He knows that they were made of golden heart, but destiny did not make good plans for them. He decided to do his part which could really change their destiny. He spoke to Saif's father.

"I have spoken to you the last time when I came here. I can help you. Please join me. What if you do not have education? I will teach you my business. Stop working as a daily labor. I can really teach you.

At least, do it for my sister. I cannot see her family in this condition"

Saif's father was not willing to take it up. He was scared of the risk involved in a costly diamond business.

Saif overheard the conversation and thought of helping his father.

"I will help you. I am educated. I can learn quickly and do a good job", Saif told his father.

Saif's father did not like it much. He knew that his son was not good at studies. So his perception was that he could not handle it. "It is diamond business. Not a game of kids. Further, you were not good at studies. Had you been, you would have got a job by this time." His father told his uncle that Saif would not be able to do it.

Saif's uncle saw a spark in the kid's eyes. He said, "Doing well at studies has nothing to do with education. Education is not about the marks you score in subjects that are taught. It is all about how capable you become as an individual. It is about how independent you can become and lead a life full of values. Karim . . . Your son has that capability. I can see it. I would even like to mention that you are an educated person even without going to a school. You have just allowed social conditioning to cover your education so deeply that you are not able to see it for yourself. But, you have unconsciously imparted it to your son. And I can see it. Help me to give a life to your son before it's too late. Whatever is the loss in the business, I would bear it. So, you need not worry."

Saif's father got convinced and allowed him to learn from his uncle. He learnt to do designs in diamonds and sell them in small shop which was purchased by his uncle. He managed the shop alone. Uncle sent him few diamonds, which he converted into beautiful jewelry and sold them. In no time, his shop was the talk of the town. Everyone came to his shop and they were thrilled by the designs he created. He sold all the diamond jewelry. His jewelry designs were famous that even people came from far off towns to purchase his designs.

Saif's father was very happy about his son's success. He remembered Saif's childhood. Saif had a zest for drawings and other paintings during his childhood. He was very creative. However, being a father who was scared of his son's future, he denied Saif doing his paintings and forced him to spend time studying. Though he repented what he did to his son's interest, he was now content that he was able to utilize his talent and became extremely successful.

Athil, who lived in the same town, continued working in the factory. Having come across Saif's success, he could not believe that a boy who was not anywhere close to his capability in studies could be so successful. He could not tolerate this. He also wanted to do what Saif did. With support from his dad, he set up a diamond jewelry shop. He got diamond supplies from his father's contacts, and started working in the shop. He employed few designers and started designing diamond jewelry. His sales were very very low. They were not even 5 % of what Saif was selling.

Athil thought the only way to success was to do what Saif did.

He started copying Saif's designs. His sales increased to certain extent. He was happy and thought that they would further improve. However, his sales started going down again. His designs were not as perfect as Saif's. Further, customers identified what's the reality and they went back to Saif who was the real creator of the designs.

Athil could not run the business. He got back to factory after realizing that diamond jewelry design was not his craft. He would never fit into it. It was only Saif who could create it."

I understood Guru's message.

"You are a unique expression of the universal soul, my son. Michael Jackson was here to express what he had to. He created something that he was born to create. That is why he could move the world. He followed his own calling. Only he could do what he did, because it was his dharma which he realized and followed without being influenced by anything else in this world.

You can't express what Michael Jackson has already done. It was his unique expression. What's yours?"

That was really a mind-blowing realization. I am here to express myself. Not anyone else. If I am doing something that others have already done, then it would not be me at all. It was time to express myself. I decided that very moment. I would never follow anyone, expect for my own calling. I will create. A great feeling again . . .

I stated, "Guru . . . Thanks once again. I have decided that I will never follow anyone. I will be myself and create what I am created for. I have decided that one day I am going to be a great musician. Also what I have decided is that, I will do so well that one day I will receive the best Musician award and travel here to show it to you as a proof of my achievement".

"That is again an output Shikar. So, will you stop once you receive the best award? Is it an end of your dream?"

I thought for a while. I got the message partially. But not completely. The Guru continued . . .

"Award is expectation out of what you do. I would say that it is nothing but a desire associated with greed. You can have a desire to conquer the world. But the desire should never be taken over by greed. Greed is one of the biggest obstacles in exhibiting peak performance. As the desire is taken over by greed, we spend time and energy in thinking about that output we are expecting and fantasizing about that output. Once we get into this mode, our mind will expect that to happen. Anything will happen only when sincere effort is put in. Most of them achieve what they expect and most of them do not. The ones who achieved will be content for few days and then a new greedy desire will make an entry. In this loop of greed and desire, the real purpose is lost. The real vision of moving the world will shift to fulfilling all the greedy desires. Further these desires are never ending and infinite. The ones, who do not achieve what they expected, will end up discontinuing their journey towards destiny. They feel that it won't work out. Actually they end up thinking that these unfulfilled greedy desires were their real destiny. Actually they changed their so called real desire to express themselves, into a petty greedy temporary output. They start redefining their capabilities and confidence levels and finally retire from the journey.

Never expect a reward for doing your duty. It's the duty assigned to you by the universal soul. In most of the religions, they call it God. So to do a job assigned by God and for what you are actually created for, you cannot expect a reward. But I assure you that the day you really start working without attachment to the output, you will see that the universe responds and makes your journey smoother than you ever thought of.

The second point I wanted to make is—you need not prove me that you have done a good job. In fact you need not prove yourself to anyone else. The only person you need to prove it to is—"YOU". You need not get an approval from anyone other than you. Be guided by our own conscience. You need not get an approval from anyone else. What does an approval from others do? It does only one thing—it strengthens your ego. Ego is the YOU, created by other people, surroundings and your reactions to the experiences you had in your life. The frame of mind which we talked about earlier. The frame of mind which acts as a reference point and obstructs the real constructive thinking process. That frame of mind is what we think we are, and what we think is the right way to be. That frame of mind which always looks for external approvals to become stronger and grow deeper roots, that we never actually know who we are in reality. We start identifying ourselves with that frame of mind. That's the ego.

So, remove the inclination of your mind to constantly satisfy others in order to strengthen this evil in you. You need not prove anything to others. Put your sincere effort in fulfilling your dharma; result will automatically come".

It was another beautiful insight. I started thinking deeply and understood that whatever we do is to satisfy only our self-framed ego. The Guru was right. How does what others think, help in realizing our purpose? In fact, it does more harm. People start giving inputs based on their own thinking. Then the process of satisfying them starts. This process of satisfying others is again to satisfy our ego—I have to be good to others and others should think only good about me. So finally, in this series of satisfying everyone else and in turn providing an assurance to our ego, we end up losing contact with our real self and landing somewhere. And that place would not be where we really wanted to be.

Assume this—you are not bothered what others think. You have the complete freedom to do whatever you want. You put your sincere efforts only on executing your craft to the best level possible. You need not show your progress to anyone else except to your commitment and your conscience. Believe that you have all the power to conquer the entire world with your craft. Believe that you can do your best every moment. Believe that you can do all of this with the infinite number of possibilities available. There is nothing that can stop you. In fact everything would start favoring you. You won't find any obstacle as a real obstacle, because you stopped judging things as right and wrong as described by the approval standards of the society. For you, everything is just a happening on your path. You think only of what you have to do.

What would come out as a result? That would be an epic. It would be a story which you need not tell others. It will be told by millions of others forever. That is the power you have."

"Which school did you go?" I asked the Guru. I was surprised by the abundant wisdom that he had. The learning that I got for the first day and the second day till then, was amazing. I really could not stop thinking that this Guru guy was fantastic. With so much of knowledge . . . Where did he gain all this from?

"The same school as you went," he said with a smile.

As usual, he confused me again. Deciding not to ask any further personal questions, I tuned myself towards learning more.

"Guru, whatever you say seems to make a lot of sense, but how do I start and execute it without even thinking of the result? Yes, there would be a lot of results if we work hard, but something solid should drive me in doing that. Please tell me a process that I can follow to achieve this."

"KARMAYOGA", in no time the Guru answered.

I was not aware of what it meant. I knew yoga. Once in a while I used to go to a hot yoga class, where we practiced a lot of body twisting and stretching postures at an elevated temperature. You return from a yoga class with a feeling which can be described as wow. Nothing less than that. So, is this also a type of exercise that I had to do? Or, is it a different form of Yoga? I remember reading about KARMAYOGA in some article related to spiritual journey. But, at that moment, I did not have any idea about it.

"I practice hot yoga. Is it another form of Yoga?" I asked the Guru. "Do I have to do some exercise or something, and would that help me in realizing my dream".

"What is your understanding of yoga? You said you practice hot yoga, what does it do to you?"

"I feel good after practicing Yoga. I feel relaxed mentally and physically and I feel that a lot of positive energy filled me up", I said.

"So, why do you feel that? Why do feel wow after your yoga class?"

I never told him that I feel wow. I was just thinking about that in my mind.

"Guru, wait a minute . . .", as I started to clarify my curiosity, "we will get to that later, my son", the Guru said sensing what I wanted to ask him.

My God! This guy was really a complete miracle. He knew everything about my past, my current state and even my thinking . . . I cannot even think of something wrong about him. Leave alone him, about anything at all. I had to be in state of complete genuineness.

"I said that we will get to that later. Stop thinking about me and please listen to me now," he said.

I reminded myself that I should not be thinking about who the Guru is till the next day, as he was anyway going to tell that.

"So, answer my question. Do you know why do you have a feeling of wow, after your hot yoga sessions?"

"I do not know," was my sincere answer.

"Let me ask you the same question in a little different way. So that you might recollect whatever you know.

Do you know what the real meaning of Yoga is?" he asked.

I started thinking of what my yoga master taught me on the first day of my yoga classes. I recollected few things.

"Yoga is an ancient practice which was born in India, more than five thousand years ago. This is a great form of exercise where we do lot of physical exercise and breathing exercises."

That was what I could remember. I was happy that I could recollect something.

"You are right till whatever you said. But your understanding of yoga is at a very superficial level. I will explain you, the deeper meaning of Yoga."

I listened very attentively; as I was really curious to know what else yoga could do to me. This would also bring me back to attend the sessions regularly. I used to skip a lot of classes.

"The word Yoga is derived from the Sanskrit word YUJ, which means union. The ultimate union of the individual soul with the universal soul is the goal of practicing Yoga. There are many paths to reach this goal. Also there are many stages in reaching the goal of Yoga. It was described by Patanjali that there are eight stages in reaching the state of ultimate union.

ASANA means posture. The practice that you are talking about is specific to this stage of the eight-fold path described by Patanjali. Also there is another stage called PRANAYAMA, which means controlled breathing. Usually these are the 2 stages which are practiced by most of the Yoga practitioners. They have a great impact on the mental and physical state of your being. They play a major role in the final destination intended by Yoga. But they alone would not help you reach the ultimate state of yoga. This state is known as SAMADHI. This is the highest state of meditation and the quest of every yogi. It is a state of joy, peace, consciousness and self-realization.

However, there are many paths of Yoga, to reach this state of SAMADHI.

HATHAYOGA is one of the forms of yoga which deals with balancing the energies and forces inside the body.

BHAKTHIYOGA is the path of prayer and intense devotion to GOD.

There are many other forms of Yoga too, out of which KARMA YOGA, is the path of YOGA which when followed for realizing your dreams, you realize that you are in the universal flow and you find your destiny that the universe has defined for you.

Karma means work. When you do selfless sincere work and have no expectations of the output, you follow this path. When you are completely occupied in doing your work tremendously well and are not bothered about any circumstances around, you follow this path. When your expression alone matters and nothing else, you follow this path. When you put all your focus on the path and not the destiny, you are on this path. When you are completely involved in learning without associating your experience with good or bad, you are on this path. When you never ever feel the importance of anyone's approval for what you do, you are on this path. When you are completely attached to the beautiful journey and enjoy each and every moment, you are on this path."

I was delighted to know this. What an insight. If I am on the path of Karma yoga, nothing seems difficult. As I am not bothered about what others think and least concerned of their approval, there is no pressure. Also, the beautiful thing is I can just focus on the effort and not the result. Amazing . . . really amazing. It is like the life where I have complete control and where I can live it king-size. Wow . . . may be that is what real living is all about. If everyone lives that way, there would be no sorrow and no war. Everyone expresses their unique talent and realize their dharma. Everyone is at peace and lives with ultimate happiness. That is what the universe seeks from each one of us.

When we are expressing ourselves completely without being influenced by anything else, we would give our 100%. And this is the state of union. There would be no separate I and the Universe. They would be one, and hence everything I want happens automatically. I need not do much and the universe does that for me. It was a real fantastic feeling.

I wanted this happiness to spread everywhere. I was thinking if what I realized, each and every person on this world realizes, it would be really great.

"I will arrange for few lectures by talking to various social welfare clubs back in my place. It would be great if you can come and provide this insight to many more people. That would make a lot more people happy. Please accept", I asked the Guru.

"Let us talk about it tomorrow, my son", the Guru said.

"But, please assure me that you will come. I really want you to help as many people as possible. Your knowledge is abundant. It cannot go wasted. Please tell me that you will surely come", I said.

"Let's talk tomorrow on this," he repeated.

One thing I observed was that the Guru was very assertive. He was very committed. As he was explaining me the concepts of life, he was completely sincere. I never felt he was unclear about anything at any point of time. He was never moved by anything I said. He portrayed a very high self-esteem. Overall, he was a great person. I decided to wait till the next day.

"Okay Guru. I will wait till tomorrow. Can you provide me guidance on how to exactly follow this path of Karma yoga? Should I just think of my passion and do whatever I can in that direction? Meaning, should I just start looking for opportunities to do the music shows in various places? How do I start?"

I accumulated all these new concepts in my mind. I learnt a lot in the last 2 days from the Guru. I made all my effort not to forget what I learnt at least till I reached my hotel room and jotted it down in my journal. Dad used to tell me that a journal would become an important part of my life.

The Guru asked, "Do you have the ability to handle a show if you get one? Are you going to do it alone or do you need support of some other people too? Do you think that you have all the skill required to do an outstanding work? Do you know what is required to do a show?"

I was not sure if I knew the answers for all those questions. But, I understood that there is a lesson coming on my way.

"First of all be clear on the outcome; on your highest goal. Once you are really clear about it and it inspires you, kindly write down. As your dad used to say, do not forget to write down something which you think as very important and you would never want to forget.

After you write down clearly what you want, it is time for mind storming. Think of all that is needed to achieve it. One you are really clear on what are the various activities or means to achieve your main purpose, note down when exactly you need each of those to happen . . . List them down. Arrange them in a sequence based on their expected occurrence in your life. That's the plan in your hand to reach your dream.

On your list, it's not what you want, that you write— it's what you would do. Because, nothing will happen if you just want it. It will happen when you do what you need to do, to receive it. Universe is ready to give whatever you need, when you sincerely do your part with a laser focus and sincere commitment.

Now, that's nothing but Karma yoga. You just work on each of the tasks, one at a time. In doing so, you put all your efforts and knowledge in doing it so well, with extreme excellence and create what is the best ever possible. You completely focus on that task without thinking of the result. Your focus and commitment is only on the executional excellence and not on the result. You invest all your energy in doing it and you create an art worth a million dollars. These you do for each and every small step on your plan with no difference in the level of commitment whatever the size of task.

While working on any task on your path, the most important factor that would drive you is the belief you have in yourself. You are the person who should believe in yourself to the best of your knowledge. This belief gets further more strengthened as you complete each and every minute task on your journey with exceptional brilliance. But to do that in the first case, you should believe that you can. This belief will help you move mountains.

And remember, you may commit a lot of errors and mistakes on the way. Do not worry about them. As the basic principle of Karma yoga says that you should not focus on the result. All you need to do is to concentrate only on the task at hand, giving it whatever possible to your maximum efficiency and capability.

So, my son, choose the path of Karma yoga and work on your dream with utmost belief."

I was very happy to hear those words from the Guru. I was feeling as if I was much more powerful and I have a capacity to do things beyond my imagination.

"It is really very inspiring Guru. But, it would be a really difficult task to change my existing mindset of focusing on results and start focusing on the journey", I wanted to get an assurance from the Guru that it would not be as difficult as I thought.

"Remember one thing", the Guru continued, "the best way to think is to understand the controls you have been provided with by this universe. The only real control you have is on the task you can do right now. You do not really have a control on the result of your task. You can just do, at this moment, whatever you want to do. You can control neither the future nor the past. All that you have a control over is on one and only one moment—the present moment.

No one in this world has the power or control on their past or future.

Close your eyes for a while and listen to what I am saying. Take 3 deep cycles of inhalations and exhalations. Be calm and breathe normally. Just focus on your breathing for couple of minutes. Let the thoughts pass by. Do not try to control them. Continue this process for some time. Just when you feel completely relaxed, feel whatever I am telling you.

- At this instance of silence, I am liberated from everything.
- I am just what I am.
- My job, my age, my house are all not me. At this moment of silence I do not have anything else . . . except this moment.

- At this moment I have a choice. A choice to do whatever I can. A choice to be happy. A choice to express myself.
- This moment is mine. I own it completely and it is my only real possession.

So, my son, liberate. Start living your dream from this moment. Do whatever is possible. The world will work for you.

❧   ❧   ❧

Open your eyes."

I really felt liberated. I was sure that I would conquer the world. And what I was very clear was that it was that particular moment I have a control over.

So each and every moment, I decided that I would live to my maximum and work on my dream sincerely.

I had few questions in my mind for which I had been looking for a proper resolution. I decided to get them clarified by asking those questions to the Guru. Who else was as sensible as this guy who is a world of wisdom? So I started:

"I have few more basic questions to ask you Guru."

"Time to leave. It's enough for today. Let us meet tomorrow morning at 6 AM."

I knew that the Guru would not oblige my request for extension of time. I said bye to him and was about to start off.

"Do not forget to write down whatever we spoke today in your journal. Time to follow dad's good practices", he smiled and walked towards his hut.

I started walking back to my hotel. I walked a little faster. I was just rewinding all the conversation we had on the second day of our meeting. I was really happy being there with the Guru. What a man he was! Those two days in India were really life changing. I was filled with positivity and certainty. What more? I had another day to go. I was more excited about the next day as it was a day of revelation of the greatest secret. Who is the Guru? How does he know so much about me than anyone else? Where did he gather all his wisdom from? The list is never ending . . .

I reached the hotel. After having my dinner I went to my room to get the journal. I would not leave even a single point of my learning from those two days. I got myself comfortable under the street lamp of the hotel on the same bench I sat the previous night.

I started writing. I consolidated the learning of both the days.

- The first and foremost realization—ultimate goal of life is HAPPINESS. Whatever we do in life is to realize this goal.
- To realize the authentic happiness in life, the path is different for each and every individual. This path

is defined by the universal soul or God whatever we name. This is the path of DHARMA.

- Dharma is the ultimate purpose of creation of each individual. Each and every person has his own Dharma which is unique. Most of the people follow or support others Dharma without expressing their own. The main reason is that they are not aware of their real purpose in life.

- The ultimate life leading philosophy which also is a way is to realize Dharma is to answer this question:

- "If I want to be happy doing what I want to do, the way I want to do and when I want to do . . . what is that I should be doing?"

- For each person, the answer to this question would be different. The day he gets the answer, it is the beginning of his journey towards destiny.

- Learn to be in silence for some time every day. Practicing silence helps us connect to the universal soul and find answers of life.

- Practice SVADHYAYA, which is a process of self-study. This helps in monitoring our progress and getting answers for the situations we face as obstacles on our journey in the divine path of realizing our Dharma.

- Be healthy. Your body is like a temple. Keep it clean and pure. Intake SATVIC food and eliminate toxins from the body. Eating right food and being healthy keeps our mind clear and calm.

- Most importantly, be in a state of positivity. Positivity is not just doing right things. It has to be extended to your thoughts and words too. When you have positive thoughts, everything around you seems to work in favor of you.

- Have a vision for your Dharma, which is so big and beyond your imagination. Do not allow the past conditioning of your mind to limit your thinking.

- Have the courage to dream big and beyond. Never bother what others say about your dream. You are a unique expression of this universal soul. It's your responsibility to be unconventional and away from the regular breed of conformity to accepted standards.

- Having your biggest vision in mind, draft all the requirements to realize it. Each and every small step required to realize your dream needs to be written down. Once the list is ready, make a note of when you want to accomplish each step. That's your plan to reach your vision.

- Practice KARMAYOGA. Do not worry about the results for each step. You have control only over the present moment and a choice to do whatever you want to do right now. You have a control neither on the past nor on the future.

- Never worry about mistakes that you do. Just think of extreme excellence on your journey and do not worry about the destination. Reaching destiny is automatic. When you give your best on what you have a control on, then results are inevitable. Nothing is good or bad. Be sincere. Do your job to the best possible. Believe in yourself and believe that you can move mountains. The world will work for you and give you whatever you want.

That was the longest content I ever wrote in my journal at one go.

I was fascinated by the learning I received and was eager to implement each of those on my return. There was a lot of connection in whatever the Guru taught on both the days. The linkage was so strong that, as I reviewed what I wrote, a single point could not be ignored. Each of the points deliberated by the Guru was so important and had a significant role in the journey to one's final destiny.

I was happy and excited about the next day. I had a list of questions which I wanted to ask the Guru for which I have been waiting for years to find answers. The most exciting thing about the next day was obvious . . .

It was 10 PM. I set alarm to 4:30 AM, and then called Simone.

Day 3:

THE AWAKENING

I was up at 4 AM, even before the alarm rang. I put the alarm off. My dad never used an alarm. He told me that if he really wanted to be up early, he never needed it. His mind did the job of an alarm and he would be up before the intended time. Our body is what we think of it. If you think you are sick, you would be. If you are happy, you would be filled with energy. You are what you think you are. It's all in your mind. My dad used to speak of lot of good things. Just like the Guru.

I got ready. I packed my luggage as I had to leave on the same day. I had to check out in the evening at 7 PM and start to Chennai via Selam. I called the taxi driver who dropped me at Semmedu on Sunday. My flight was at 11:30 PM back home.

I dialed the reception to inform that I would be vacating my room that day. But I wanted to keep my luggage in reception, so that I can leave directly after I return from the mountains. I wanted to save as much time as possible, as I wanted to learn as much as possible from the Guru that last day. I reached the reception and settled the bill. It was 5 AM.

I started walking towards the mountains. That evening at 4 PM, I had to collect the medicine for my uncle. So, I decided that I would not waste any time in resolving all the queries I had before that time. It was a strange feeling.

I felt so close to the trees, the mountains, the Guru and the purity of that place. It had become an integral part of me. The Guru rightly said that when we are in silence and purity, we are one with everything. I was really going to miss that place. It has given my life back to me. I had developed a bonding with that place that could not be described in words. It was a lovely place.

I felt immense power as I walked towards my destiny. I was a completely changed man. I was filled with so much of confidence that I would definitely make a difference in this world.

I reached the place at 5.45 AM. I sat on a rock and was waiting for the Guru to arrive. I started thinking how beautiful life is when we are living our dream and choose to be happy at every moment.

"Nothing is permanent in this world, my son. As you know, we have control only over this moment and only this moment is permanent. So learn that, to be happy forever, you should conquer each and every moment completely.

Anyways, congratulations on starting your true journey. I am happy that now, you have got everything to lead an independent and purposeful life. You have chosen the right path, Shikar. It's time to move on with the same zeal in your life ahead."

"Thanks a lot Guru. It is all because of you that I have got my life back. Now I have the confidence that I can realize my Dharma at any cost and nothing can stop me in doing that."

"My son," continued the Guru, "it is not about achieving at any cost, but achieving whatever you want by being sincere and righteous to your conscience."

"Also, I would like to make one thing very clear to you Shikar. Remember that there is no one in this world who can teach you anything. Anyone can just tell you what they know. What happens then is that, it is your consciousness which helps you understand that concept. Now, no one knows how this process of understanding takes place. The universe is very mysterious. It has got everything in abundance. Whenever required, your individual intelligence gets in touch with the abundant knowledge already existing in the pool of universal intelligence.

In actual, you are one with the universe. So, where is the process of learning? You are just using your own intelligence."

I tried to interpret what the Guru just explained. I reprocessed it in my mind. I understood to a great extent. But not completely.

"Don't struggle with something you are not able to get. You will get it when it is required," the Guru said.

"The universe has given us few powers that we do not realize. I would like to explain you the most important powers of the universe that we possess. Each and every individual soul has these powers. The individual who makes complete use of these powers will become capable of creating his own destiny. After explaining those powers, I will answer all the questions you wanted to ask me."

The Guru explained me few powers of universe that day. "My son, please remember that each of these powers is available for us and provides us the support to reach our destiny.

The **first** and foremost power is the **POWER OF PRESENCE**. The power of presence can also be called as the power of mindfulness. You might be thinking that it is a very simple thing but it is not. It is the most powerful of all. Let me explain you what it is. A newly born child has the capability to grasp each and everything. We are a particle of the Universal soul and have the power of the universe. At that stage, as a child, we have infinite capability of creation. As we grow; this capability of creation is used little by little and finally we become an independent adult. It is a fantastic achievement to grow into an independent adult who can do everything on his own. But, the sad part is that most of us lose the capability of creation as we grow. We lose it not because we grow up, but because we do not use it. Anything used will grow and strengthen. We start aligning to specifications set by society and start conforming to it. This becomes a habit and by the time we grow, we move completely to a mechanical state than the creative state. The basic reason is not using the power of presence.

A child is not worried about the past or the future. It just enjoys being in that moment COMPLETELY. This is what helps the child to do things which we feel are nothing less than miracles. A child is alert to take everything. It does each activity with so much of awareness. It is excited and passionate about doing things. Not about what would happen after the activity is completed. Being mindful at every moment comes with a lot of practice. Meditation helps you to a great extent to master this. So, always be mindful and completely present in every moment and be ready to receive what the universe has got to offer you.

The second important power is the **POWER OF BELIEF**. I already spoke to you about this yesterday. The power of belief is the vehicle which would carry you to your destination. As you believe in yourself completely, you create an intention in the universal field. This means that you create and emit the energy, which would actually make the universe work for you and would bring you whatever you intended to receive. It is very essential to strengthen this power of belief. As I said, it is the vehicle which would create circumstances favorable to you on the path which you travel and reach your destiny.

To strengthen this power of belief, there are two ways. The first one is the habit of action and the second one is the tool of affirmation. The first one is very important my son. You should take action every moment according to your plan. Each and every time you take an action you fuel your belief. As you fuel you belief, and keep working with focus, the universe will give you what you want. This in turn fuels your belief again. Action is the best affirmation that you use as a fuel to strengthen your power of belief. Affirmation is a simple yet powerful technique. It is about telling yourself everyday what is that you need exactly. This is a process of feeding your mind with the intention and believing that it will happen. As someone said, believe that you can move the mountains and you will.

The next universal power available for you is the **POWER OF BEING YOURSELF**. This power is all about being YOU. As I said earlier, you are a unique expression of the universal soul. The universe has created you for a purpose. To live your purpose, it becomes more important to be YOU first. Being YOU means, being aligned to your consciousness. At any point of time, you make a decision based on your conscience—purely based on only your conscience. Your conscience knows what is right and what is not. Believe in it. Rely on it. When you do this on a continuous basis, your self-esteem grows. Your confidence grows. You will grow spiritually, and you will become what you are truly supposed to become. You will realize your Dharma.

The next power available to you is my most favorite power. It is the **POWER OF SILENCE**. This power for me is nothing but a divine connection. When you are silent, you connect to the universal cosmic flow and you feel one with everything. Silence means not just to stop speaking. Silence is the silence of words, actions and thoughts. When you are calm and silent, as you experienced, you will get answers from the universal soul. Every day, I insist that you make it a practice to be silent for some time. Even five minutes of silence will make a huge difference in your life. You can seek answers for your life. You can get solutions for the issues you face. You will get ahead on your path towards destiny with clarity which is the primary feature in leading a fantastic life. In the busy life that we are leading today, we never even think of silence. Most of them can't be silent even for a single moment as they are addicted to noise. The noise in the outside world, and also the noise within. They do not even appreciate the need for silence and due to the addiction to noise; they feel it is a waste of time.

The moment of realization comes when they either connect with nature or see a small child or listen to a soulful music. Whenever they connect to something pure and natural, they identify the inclination towards silence and realize its importance. This sort of encounter also helps people to start their spiritual journey.

POWER OF COINCIDENCES, is another power of universe, which seems to be little miraculous. It talks about each and every incident that happened in your life. If you start thinking back, in your life, every incident has played its part in shaping what you are today. Each and every moment that you lived, and the choice that you made, had an impact on your life. Just think of this event. You met me here, in these mountains. Never in your wildest dreams, would you have imagined this incident would happen. You are here to buy medicine as required by your aunt. Your aunt wanted medicine for your uncle who has a health problem. Your aunt came to know about this place from her friend. Had she not discussed about your uncle with her friend, she would not have known this place. So, you are here. Assume that you got the medicine the day you reached here. You would have returned with the medicine and never met this lecture guy. Multiple events link that occurred finally created this event that made you meet me.

Now, this event, which is our meeting, sure would change your life into a different direction all together. See how important the events and incidents that happen in your life are. At each of these moments when the incidents occurred, you had a choice to choose one of the multiple possibilities available at your service. Each and every choice made at each and every moment matters. Had you given some reason to your aunt, as you were completely not willing to come here, you would have not met me. You made a choice to come. When the Pundit was not available, you could have made a choice of returning, instead of waiting for next three days. But, you chose to stay. If you had returned, we would have not met.

See, how important the choice you make at each and every moment mattered so that you could meet me. The universe has worked for your good. It is not because of anyone else. It is just because of you. It is because of your strong intention in the subconscious state of mind, where there is a strong need for your spiritual evolution. You are not aware of it completely. But, it is only because of you that you are here and we are meeting each other.

The person who is in a blissful state lives in every moment completely. If you want to be in the right path, make a right choice every moment and every time. Be completely aware of the happening and be present fully. And remember, the situations that happen are a consolidated result of the choices that you made.

Make your choice to live today and appreciate the power of coincidences. Live every moment and make the right choice every time. Again remember, right means not the accepted right as per social standards—right to your own conscience.

The last power that I would like to share with you is the **POWER OF GRATITUDE**.

Gratitude means appreciating and being thankful to the incidents and people linked to those incidents in your life.

As I told you when I explained the previous power, which is the power of coincidence, each and every incident will shape our lives. Every moment is an experience which creates a sort of mind patterns, and these patterns would be the basis for the next incidents. Okay . . . let's not get into too much details of it. Let me try to explain it in short.

It is important to revisit the experiences that we had and then, say thanks to them. Basically, you are trying to change your mind pattern. You are trying to convert everything into a good pattern. I know that you are still not very clear on how to follow this. Let me give you an example. Assume that you had a bad experience in your office. A colleague of yours has misbehaved with you. At that moment, you get angry which is completely understandable. But the damage this incident has caused will be substantial. It has created a mind pattern in you. This mind pattern is used as a reference thereafter. Hope you remember our earlier discussion on social conditioning of our mind, which is later used as a reference. Next time you see that person; this reference mind pattern provides a prejudice which is nothing but a bad feeling again. You have another bad experience, as you anyways expected it. Now, this in turn creates another pattern which overlaps and makes the earlier pattern stronger. Thus, the negative pattern becomes stronger and stronger. Resultant is that, the feeling of hate is consuming the place of most powerful positive feeling which is love. As it grows further, it consumes further more space which is meant for love. Over a period you become a negative minded person. You would have heard people using that term—Negative minded person.

Oh my God! See the influence of a small spat in office in shaping your life.

There is a way. The way is to practice gratitude. All that you need to do is to take your journal and write all the experiences you had that day. They should include both good and bad experiences. After you complete writing, go through the list one by one and say, "I am thankful that I had this experience today". When you come across a bad experience like the one we talked about, you can still say that you are thankful that you had that experience. You are thankful because you had the learning. You are thankful because you helped that person vent out his or her anger. You are happy and thankful just for the experience. And finally, you say to yourself, "I forgive myself and the other person. I understand that people are different and each person has his or her own opinion. No one is incorrect from their own perspective. Everyone has a point which makes it right for them. I respect that."

Actually, there is no good or bad experience. There is no good or bad person. From today, make a resolution that you would not judge anything. The judgment you make is not available anywhere in the reality. It is only in your mind and is an illusion. Catch yourself judging a person or situation and when you do this tell yourself, "Every person is different and unique and every incident is an experience. Still I have a choice to have my opinion and be happy whatever may be the incident or situation. I recognize that the judgment is only in my mind and nowhere in the world outside me."

By practicing this gratitude habit every day, you will release the old patterns and be ready to take things as they are, without referring any predefined patterns of your mind.

So, these are the major powers that the universe has made available to you. I am saying that they are available to you. I am not saying that you have them. These powers cannot be received or used by all. It is available only for the chosen few who are sincerely working to make their way to their destiny—Dharma realization.

All these powers are interdependent. You cannot ignore one power and decide to use or avail just a couple of them. Work sincerely and earn the powers and their fruits completely.

This is what I wanted to tell you. Now, you can ask the questions you have in your mind."

I was silent for a while. In fact I was trying to digest the learning on powers that the Guru just explained in detail. It was so great to listen to him and those concepts were really so powerful. I repeated the list of all powers in my mind so that I register them and then can make place for them into my journal.

I took out the paper I brought with me, which had a list of questions. These were the questions for which I was searching answers.

"Guru", I continued, "I have a list of questions with me. These are the questions for which I have always been searching for answers. You would have touched upon few of these topics during your mentoring for the last 2 days that we met and to a great extent even on today. I still need clarity on many questions which remain either unanswered or I have got multiple answers when I asked different people. I believe in you completely. You have triggered a change in my life for which I cannot repay the price in my entire lifetime. I think you are a great person, great friend and mentor for me. Whatever, are the answers that you give me for these questions that I am going to ask you, I would take them to be the final answers. Because, I believe in your wisdom and I respect you as my mentor."

"Shikar", the Guru replied, "as I already told you, you can listen to whatever anyone tells you. But, the final decision on any action or belief system that you create should completely be based on yourself. You cannot blindly let others create the acceptance standards in your mind. Then there would not be any difference between you and a person who always conforms to the acceptance norms as per the society. This is the first and foremost thing that you need to follow. This is the foundation for bringing out the independent and unique person out of you."

I understood the Guru's point very clearly. This is what he was emphasizing from the day I met him. But, I surely wanted to understand his views on the questions I had. That would mean a lot to me. I always wanted to hear answers that are sensible—like the Guru's concepts.

"Sure Guru," I said, "I would definitely follow what you said. But I am keen to know the answers for these questions from your perspective. I assure you that I would definitely not take the answers provided by you for granted. I would process them in my mind and then take what I feel as right to my conscience. In these few days of my interaction with you, I always felt that you think the way I do, when I am at my best state of mind. So your view point for me makes a lot of sense. I request you to please answer my questions."

The Guru said, "You need not request me my son. I am here to help you. My purpose of meeting you is to help you out of your life which was going nowhere. I am here to put you on the right path. I was just giving you a word of caution. I will be there for you anytime to answer any of your questions. You can ask me as many questions as you want to. I will answer them."

I was obliged by what the Guru said. It gave me a great feeling of happiness and security when the Guru said that he would help me whenever required. I decided to make him my mentor for my life. I decided to visit him every year or whenever I feel that I am going off-track.

"Thanks a lot Guru. I am extremely happy to hear what you just said. It means a lot to me. I will come here at least once a year. I request you to be my mentor for life. Please accept to be my mentor and help me to lead a purposeful life."

"I am with you always. Do not worry about it. And coming to the point of meeting once a year; let's discuss on that at the end of the day."

The Guru, as usual left some suspense. I knew that thinking about it would only waste the valuable time that we had together. So, without wasting any further time, I started asking the questions.

What is Success?

A fulfilled life. Now, the meaning of fulfillment varies from person to person. Most of the people mistake the meaning of fulfillment as attaining all the material things like car, house, bank balance etc., these material desires are never ending. They keep growing upon fulfillment too. A young man dreamt of getting a good job after his education. He finally landed up in a job which was better than what he dreamt of. He was satisfied. After few days, he felt that he should buy a small car. That was his next dream. He worked hard and got a promotion. He bought a car with the increased pay. He was satisfied again, but only for few days. He now wanted to own a house. He worked hard and finally managed to take a loan from a bank. He got a two bedroom flat. He was satisfied. But, again he was happy only for few days. Now, he wanted a big car. His desires never ended. After each of the desires got fulfilled, the next one was ready knocking at his door.

This is how life goes on for most of us. We mistake success for possession of all the material things in this world. The process of attaining this type of success is never ending. When the life ends, most of the people will have everything that they ran behind, but, finally they realize that they did not live at all. Few of us on this materialistic journey of success, are fortunate to realize the real meaning of success, which is LIVING each and every moment with real fulfillment.

Where does this state of real fulfillment come from? The answer is—When you live up to your Dharma. This is what gives you real fulfillment. When you express your

Dharma completely, you live completely. As I already told you, each and every person on this earth is created to do something. That something is unique for each and every person. The moment he realizes his "WHAT" of life, he starts his real journey of success. That's the inner calling. Once he gets the inner calling, and he starts living his purpose, every moment is successful. As long as he lives his Dharma, the definition of success and failure no more exist. He just lives a life of fulfillment and happiness.

How does one know what is his purpose or the so called Dharma? Are there any ways by which he can identify what he is made for?

Identification of one's Dharma is a continuous process. It is an evolution of your true self. The trigger for this realization process can be different for different individuals. Those who are blessed with freedom and independence during their childhood, most of the time realize their dharma without much of an additional effort. A child when is born is so pure and is having capability in abundance. The potential that any child has is infinite. Slowly, the child turns into an adult with a character. This process of character formation has its own effect in the process of realization of Dharma. For instance, if a child is helped with everything and told what he has to do under what circumstances, the possibility of his unique expression gets buried and there would be a number of layers which are laid by social conditioning process.

Take another example. Assume that a child is just supported ONLY when really required, and not controlled as per the need of parents. Assume that the child is given freedom and independence, with lots of love. He is always allowed to express himself and not forced to express his parents or teachers or neighbors through him. This forms a beautiful foundation for his future. This foundation allows him to be always in peace, fearless, and in sync with the universal intelligence. So, when he grows up, he need not put an additional effort to do what he wants to do. He would be so independent that he would always be on track to live his Dharma. This support is the major change required in parenting and education system.

The child who is always controlled needs to put in a lot of effort to come to his real path of destiny. Most of them even fail to realize that there is a need for this effort, till the end of their lives.

There are few other ways that form a trigger to realize the true self and right path. A feeling of discomfort when you are not on the right path arises from within. This is referred as INNER CALLING. No one knows from where this trigger comes from. No science can prove the point of initiation of this inner calling. When this discomfort increases, it directs you to take actions that would put you on your path. When you are expressing yourself with the expression you are created for, there would be no discomfort. You would be in a flow that is close to divinity filled with total peace, contentment and energy. You would not feel that you are working hard. You would be enjoying whatever you are doing and time would cease to have any meaning.

Also, another trigger to start the search for Dharma comes up when you come across something unexpected in life. Loss of dearest ones, diagnosis of terminal illness etc., are examples of such incidents. Everything seems to stop suddenly, when incidents like these happen. We would have never expected something like that. Everything seems to have changed drastically due to such events for which we would not be prepared. Then we start thinking of the real life. Questions like, what is the real meaning of life, come up. Then it creates the zeal to find our real self rather than just doing something and passing the days.

So, my son, there are many ways, in which the point of trigger occurs. Whatever may be the trigger, the moment it happens, the moment the inner calling arrives . . . your life begins.

What is Peace?

Peace is a state of being. It is beautiful state of being.

When you are completely in the present and when you are totally mindful of your activity, you are in peace.

Usually, people feel that peace is time bound and external. This means, peace is available only during the time when there is complete silence around you. For example, you are here in these mountains. There is no noise like in the cities with fast paced life. So, you feel that you are in a peaceful atmosphere and you will have peace till you are here. Tonight, after you return, you will not be in peace again. You will miss this place. You will tell your friends that you had been to a beautiful place which was very peaceful. So, you feel that peace is attached to the external world. In actual, peace is something related to the internal world; the world within you. There is no world without you. You see it with your eyes and label it as you feel. So, you see peace in a silent place like these mountains and feel that within you. In fact, everything is happening inside you. You are seeing with your eyes and interpreting with your mind and feeling the happiness within you. Which means the entire process is within you. There is not much role played by these mountains. It is you who made a choice of labeling it as peaceful.

I would not say that the mountains have done nothing. The mountains have provided you the basic foundation for choice of thought, better interpretation and reaction. But, the most important thing is that there were no other distractions in these mountains. This means, you were focused. You were completely present without any external source of distraction. Internally you were totally mindful of what you are doing. So, the root cause of your peace here is not the external factors, but, the absence of distraction. Usually, your mind is filled with thousands of thoughts flashing—either about the past or the future. These thoughts are the distractions for your divine connection with the source of peace. As you become focused and as you stop worrying about past or future, you minimize your thoughts. The lesser the number of thoughts, greater the space you create for experiencing the present moment which has abundance of peace. The state of being that connects you to your source.

Stop looking for peace externally. As you create silence in your inner world by minimizing the thoughts that flash without invitation, you reach the peaceful state. You will be in peace not only when you sit alone, but also with thousands of people around you. Because you chose to be in present. Because you chose to be totally aware and mindful of each and every activity you do. Because you chose to be peaceful.

That was a great point. But how do we practice being silent within? It is not so easy for anyone like me to reduce the number of thoughts, as we have different experiences everyday which gives rise to many thoughts.

Like how you do physical exercise to tone up your body, you should do exercise to silence your mind. Practice of Meditation is the well-known technique that trains your mind to have minimal thoughts.

For most of them meditation practice seems to be a complex one and many a time people feel that it is possible to attain a meditative state only after years of practice. We need to stay in a 'so called peaceful place' and practice it for years. But this is a misconception. Meditation definitely has few stages, the final stage being SAMADHI, as I explained earlier. But it is not as difficult to practice as many think of it.

Meditation is being in silence. Just sit for some time, around 10 to 20 min, in a comfortable position. Keep your back straight. Start inhaling and exhaling with your nostrils, keeping your mouth closed. Bring your attention to your breathing. Be completely relaxed while practicing. Your mind might wander and it might start oscillating between the thoughts about past and future. It is absolutely fine. Just observe the thoughts. As you realize you are not in the present, you bring your attention back to your breathing. Practice this way for few days with 10 to 20 min every day, and you will see that the number of thoughts start to reduce. You have more space for creativity and expression. This is meditation.

So, my son, as you practice it every day, you understand that you get deeper into the meditation and finally reach a state of complete silence and alertness. As this state you feel a sense of joy. You feel you are in the flow; the universal flow. This stage is the goal of Meditation. It is known as SAMADHI. You would recognize that you are one with the universe.

Continuous practice of Meditation will lead you to eternal peace.

How important is Physical health and what is the role that it plays on our path towards destination?

Our body is like a temple. Keeping it healthy is an important means in which we can reach the state of silence and peace. When our physical health is good, we feel happy and our mind will be peaceful. We should keep our body clean and healthy. Your mental state is to a great extent dependent on your physical health condition. Mind and body are not different. They are interdependent. Techniques like Yoga are focused on strengthening and alignment of mind and body. Yoga involves techniques which makes us mentally stable and physically fit.

Not only Yoga, even other physical exercises like running, walking, weight training also focus to some extent on mind training. When you are doing any form of physical exercise, the mind is focused on your body for most of the duration of practice. This automatically brings down the number of thoughts and increases peace. Also, what you focus on strengthens. So, the part of your body where you focus and work on will grow fit and healthy.

As our mind becomes stable and peaceful, and our body has the fitness and energy, it complements you to lead your way towards destiny.

Further, the only means for your soul to express your Dharma in this physical world is your body. So, it is your responsibility to be healthy and take care of your body.

People like me feel happy when we are connected with nature. Why?

My son, you belong to nature. So you feel happy and connected to your true self. In our urban world, we have a very limited access to nature. Access to nature is a door to access the origin to which you belong. It is recommended to spend some time in nature as the silence of nature has the power to speak to your soul.

Being in nature helps you connect to the universal soul. Whatever is in nature is pure and in original state. Hence we are able to connect to that originality, which is nothing but our own originality. We all emerge from the same source. Due to various reasons, as we grow up, we miss the touch with our origin. But nature has not. So, we see our own origin when we see nature. We in fact reconnect to where we should have been.

It is not just nature, that make us reconnect to the universal soul; our origin. Anything pure for that matter helps that connection bounce back and knock our souls for some time. Another such means would be a small child. We feel happy when we see a child. The simple reason is that the child is so pure. It is real and not yet conditioned by societal standards. Purity means connection to origin. So, when we see a small child, we feel happy from within. The reason—knock on the door of origin.

Another example is music. You said that you wanted to be a musician. Though everyone does not want to be a musician, most of us love listening to music. Any form of music, when it is pure, brings that divine connection within us. We feel peaceful. We feel happy. Again the reason is purity and originality. Anything pure knocks the door.

What is Spirituality?

For many people, being spiritual is following some religion deeply. This is not correct. Spirituality is not about religion. It is about one self. It is about self-realization. In fact, any person who either follows a religion or does not follow any religion can grow spiritually. Spiritual growth is nothing but a progressive self-realization. The more you know yourself and the inner world within you, the more you grow spiritually. In fact, the final stage of spiritual growth is the feeling of oneness with everything. You will realize that you are one with the world.

The person, who is on the path of spirituality, will work internally. He does what is right to his consciousness. He does not feel the need to prove anything to anyone. He always is in peace, whatever the external situation is. He is not worried about what others think of him. He is fearless. He is always calm and he glows with the touch of universal power in him. He realizes his dharma and lives a fulfilled life.

In the process of spiritual growth, one will understand that life and death are just happenings of the greater life. One, who is spiritually mature, does not fear death. It is just the loss of the physical presence. But he believes the soul never dies. He lives even after death in the form of dharma that he fulfilled and left for others to carry forward for generations. He lives forever.

I took a pause. What the Guru just said was something beyond normal. It was very powerful and it took some time for me to come back to normalcy. So, after few minutes, I asked my next question.

Why is it so important to be positive all the time? What is the role that positivity plays in our life?

It is not important to be positive all the time. What is important is to accept the situation as it is. Accepting a situation means having complete understanding that what you can control is nothing else other than yourself, at any moment. So, what you have is a choice to accept the situation and to react in the way you want. The external situation does not change whatever you do. The moment is happening. You have the only choice of how you want react to it. This is real positivity.

When we accept things as they are and make a choice to be calm and think of what best can be done to have a different outcome next time that is when we act with positivity. A person who is calm, peaceful and fearless is always capable of taking the right decisions with a high level of confidence. This is what is being positive all about.

Assume a situation where some dearest one has passed away. You cannot tell yourself to be positive and not grieve. Of course accept that the person has left the body and undergo the process of grieving. You have to release the emotion and let it flow. Once the grieving process is over, after few days or months do something that helps the person live even after he left his physical body. Work on the unfulfilled wishes to give peace to that soul.

Being positive helps strengthen the power of belief that we spoke about earlier. As you are positive, you attract positive situations in life. What you think is what you are. So to be a positive person, you should have positive thoughts. Be extremely positive about the dreams you have. This will attract all the possibilities to realize your dream. Dream big. Believe completely. Attract possibilities. Realize your purpose. Live fully.

When is the right time to start working on our dreams or to walk on our journey of Dharma realization?

Now. Right now. At this moment. You can start living your dream from this very moment. Nothing can stop you from doing what you want other than YOU. People make the mistake of creating a target date to start working on their dream. You start working on your dream the moment you realize it. Plan for it. Take some small step today; each day—it is definitely possible. As you take a small step every day your get closer to your dream.

Each and every day is an opportunity to learn something new. Remember that to give your best possible outcome, you need to work on yourself in the direction of your dream. So, nothing can stop you from learning something every day and enhancing your knowledge. People say that knowledge is power. Yes it is. It is the real power that leads you to your destination. Gain as much knowledge as possible in your craft and deepen your skill so much that each and every step that you execute is outstandingly brilliant.

Focus on one step at a time. It can be very small. But execute it with excellence. If learning something in your craft is on your plan, do it. Do it with so much sincerity that the universe recognizes your focus and starts creating the path by showing you more possibilities. The universe responds to your sincerity. The universe responds to your focused effort. It responds. So, never plan with date that starts somewhere in future. The time is NOW!

Who is God according to you?

For me God is in the silence. Because in silence there is nothing. And this nothing is the source of everything. So, for me God is nothing and everything at the same time. In the silence, there is a complete presence. There is a divine experience. For me, that experience of divinity is God.

We had no religions few thousands of years ago. Once, these religions came into existence, many belief systems evolved along with each religion. So, the followers of each religion have a lot of belief in their own systems. For them, that sincere belief is God. That sincere belief with which they pray helps them experience the presence of God. And when they ask for something with that powerful belief, favorable circumstances are created and they receive what they want.

God can be seen anywhere, nowhere and everywhere. For me God is a power that can never be defined in words. Power that can just be felt.

I listened to each and every answer the Guru provided very carefully and the essence of each of the answers sank into me slowly.

But, the most important question still remains unanswered; the answer that I was waiting to hear desperately for last three days. Finally, I asked him.

"Guru, I admire your patience. The answers that you gave for my questions are really eye openers and I would carry the essence of those throughout my life. Also, I want to thank you so much for the last three days. The way you mentored me has given me a new direction in life; the right direction. Your lessons are amazing and I can never forget them. I promise you that I will follow them throughout my life and realize my Dharma."

"Please do not promise me. Promise to you," the Guru said without waiting even a second.

"Okay . . . Okay. Apologies. I missed it. I promise only to myself. I will keep my promise. Now, I have a final question."

"Please ask me my son", the Guru said waiting for my question.

I put up my question, "Who are you? Why did you help me so much for the past three days?"

"Shikar, the time is 3:30 PM; it is time for you to collect the medicine. Why don't you go and collect it? We can discuss this upon your return," the Guru said.

"I do not think that you would take more than a couple of minutes to just tell me who you are!"

"No, my son, it would require more time to explain you. So, please listen to me. Go to the Pundit and get your medicine. We will discuss upon your return."

I had never told the Guru that I should be collecting the medicine at 4 PM. He knew it. How . . . ? the answer was waiting for my return from the Pundit. I have waited for so long. I told myself that I will have the patience to wait for one more hour. In fact, I had no choice. The Guru would not listen to any further request.

"Okay", I said, "I will be right back after I collect my medicine. You can rest in your hut till then."

The Guru smiled and said, "Sure my son, your answer will wait for you. Take care. Make it fast. Do not miss your flight at 11:30 PM. You have to leave at 7 PM from the hotel at any cost. Otherwise you will miss the flight."

"Sure, I will make it fast".

As I walked towards the Ayurveda center to meet the Pundit, my mind was still thinking about the Guru's teachings. All the learning I received during those three days in India would be the turning point in my life. What I never imagined in my dreams happened there. What an impact a small coincidence can have on our life? I was very happy. But all the more excitement was about who the Guru was. I could not wait to return to his hut in the mountains.

I reached the Ayurveda Center. I entered and saw the person whom I met on Sunday.

"Has Mr. Pundit Ram Rajan returned?" I asked him.

"Yes. Of course. He has returned. Please take your seat."

I felt relieved that Pundit was available. I waited there sitting on a sofa made of cane. There was a Carnatic music being played in the center. The aroma of that place was so pleasant. I was relaxed.

"How can I help you sir?", the Pundit asked as he entered the area where I was waiting.

"Punditji, I came here for a medicine to help my uncle get relieved of his skin disease. I heard from my aunt that the medicine to cure that peculiar skin disease is available only in your Ayurveda center. Can you please help me with that medicine?" I asked and explained him more details about my uncle's illness.

"Wait for 30 min. I will prepare the medicine and bring it for you," he said.

"30 minutes? Can you make it faster?" I asked.

"You waited for 3 days for this medicine, my dear boy. Why are you not able to wait for just 30 minutes more?"

"I need to go and meet a friend of mine before I leave. Please help me Punditji", I said.

"See . . . If a medicine needs to be prepared, it will take it's time for right preparation. It is not just putting the required ingredients and mixing them up. It is the state of mind of the preparer that is more important. There should be a lot of positivity and a powerful intention which are the key ingredients to prepare the right medicine. It is not just about the physical ingredients my son, it more of the intention! Please wait."

"Why are people in this place so unique?" I thought, and had no choice other than waiting for him to complete the preparation. I waited on the bench placed outside in the garden in front of the Ayurveda Center. As I waited, I started thinking of the time I spent with the Guru. The Guru became really very close to my heart. The person who changed my life forever . . .

"The medicine is ready. Punditji is calling you to collect it," a person from the center informed.

"What is your name?" asked the Pundit. Wondering why he is asking that question, I answered, "My name is Shikar, and I have come down from California."

"Shikar, you seem so restless. I am happy to help you if you need anything. You are from a far off place. Is there anything that is bothering you here? Let me know if you need anything my boy." The Punditji offered his warm support. I was so pleased with the way he responded. It was so nice of him to extend his support to a Customer beyond his normal service. I felt very good about it.

"I met a new friend here, who has become very close to my heart in the last three days of stay. Actually, I was very upset when you left for some work even upon our confirmation that we would be here to collect the medicine. But, what my dad used to tell me has come true. He always told me that whatever happens in life is for your own good. It is just about how you take it. So, during my extended stay here, what happened to me is nothing less than the best encounter that I could have ever imagined. I met a person, who has taught me the most amazing concepts that would help me lead my life to meet the purpose of my existence to its maximum."

"We never know what life has destined for us", he said, "I am sorry about my absence. There was a miss on our internal communication and I could not be here for you. My apologies."

"That is absolutely okay Punditji. In fact I spoke very rudely to your person the other day. I should be sorry for my behavior."

"No problem", he said with a gentle smile.

I thanked him, paid the money at the bill counter and left immediately. I walked as fast as I could. I had to reach the mountain and talk to the Guru. I had to know who he was. And I had to reach the airport on time. I walked for the next fifteen minutes, with a feeling which I would not be able to describe. I was excited, tensed, happy etc . . .

I was in the final turning point which would take me to the Guru's place. I increased my pace. I was almost running. And I was finally there . . .

The Guru was not there on the rock where he usually sat. I thought he would be in his hut and turned towards the hut. To my surprise, there was no hut . . . I was shocked as I could not believe my own eyes. The Guru and his hut which were very much there about an hour ago were not there anymore.

I went to the exact spot where the hut existed before and checked if there are any traces of the same. But there was not a single trace that showed the existence of the hut. The ground was so clear as if nothing ever existed there before. How could someone leave a place in such a short span of time? In an hour's time, how can anyone shift his entire house and leave no trace of even its existence?

The time was 5.30 PM. I had to leave the place in an hour and a half. I had to leave from the mountains latest by another one hour. What should I do? Should I wait for him hoping that he would come? After seeing the place, I lost the faith that he would ever come back. I had two questions for him. Who was he and whether he would be my mentor . . . ? I sat there on my favorite rock for few minutes to be in silence and think of my next best step.

Why did the Guru leave without telling me anything? How I can find who he is? What should I do now? Various questions filled me up . . . Then I thought of seeking help from someone to find out details about the Guru or at least a clue to reach him. I had very less time. I thought of the receptionist in the hotel. Whether he would be able to help me? I just rewound my conversation with the Guru. When

I first asked him who he was, he had told me that people call him GURU. That is when I started addressing him that way. So, being a person of such a great wisdom, he would be famous in that area. So, anyone should be able to tell me who he was. This meant that, the receptionist at the hotel was not a wrong choice. However, what pulled me back was the lack of time. So, the choice I would make should be the best and accurate. I thought of few more options, and the people who came into my mind were the restaurant owner at the hotel, the boy at the massage center and finally the Punditji. Yes . . . the best choice was the Punditji. He was an elderly man and he also offered me help. He was so humble. It was time I had to make a decision on my choice of person who can lead me to the Guru's identity. It was 6:00 PM.

I decided that I would rely on the Pundit. So, I headed towards the Ayurveda Center. I started running as fast as I could. It was my last hour at Kolli hills. I had to find the most important answer. I consolidated all the energy I had and rushed as speedily as I could. I reached the Ayurveda Center at 6:15 PM.

"I have to talk to Punditji", I asked the assistant at the Center. Impeccably came the answer, "Sorry sir, we are closing the center for the day. Punditji is seeing his last patient and he would take another 15 minutes to complete the treatment. After which, we would be closing for the day."

"My meeting with the Punditji is very important. Please help me", I pleaded.

"Sorry Sir, you can come tomorrow morning at 8 AM."

I did not have another choice. I had to meet the Pundit at any cost. I was not sure if I would get the answer. But, I decided that I would believe and give that try. How do I meet him?

"Look Sir. I am leaving this place in another 45 minutes. I have come from California. I came here for your help. An hour ago, I met your Punditji to collect some medicine. He said that he would be happy to help me. Please let him know that I am waiting for him. I am sure that he would take out his time to help me. Please do this favor." The assistant seemed to be convinced.

"I understand that you are in some trouble sir. I will help you with what you asked. But I cannot break the rules of our Center. Punditji will be extremely focused on his work while he treats his patients. He would not like anyone impede his work. You have to wait till he completes treating this last patient. I will pass on your message immediately after his work. That is the best possible help from my side."

"Thank you so much," I said, and waited hoping that the last patient would come out as soon as possible. It was

6.20 PM. Each and every minute was so important for me. It passed as if each minute was an hour. There were times when the same time passed so fast. When we were on a holiday, we felt that the time passed so fast. We wanted to it to be still. That same TIME, which passed so fast, was now moving so slow and was almost still. How could this happen? The Guru said that everything is in the way you see it. Does this mean that even time is not real? Does it really exist or it is in our mind? . . . It was 6.24 PM.

The assistant saw me. He told me, "I know that you are restless because of something which is bothering you very much. Anything outside you cannot be controlled by you. Have patience sir. Believe and everything will be alright. You will get what you want."

Those words really gave me a bit of relief. I understood how much it matters when someone supports you morally. You will have a feeling of belonging and oneness. It was 6.26 PM.

I heard the creak of the door opened by an old lady, who was the last patient. She was in her nineties. She could barely walk. The Punditji supported her till the door and from there the assistant took her. I remembered my grandmother when she was old. I did not regret waiting. I felt her treatment was definitely superior to my requirement of being there.

I stood up after seeing the Pundit, so that I could get his attention. And I succeeded. While he turned back towards his room after leaving the lady, he saw me.

"Yes Shikar. You were supposed to leave today. What brought you here? You look anxious about something. Do you need to know something from me?"

"Yes, Punditji. I need a help from you. I came here for some information. It is of utmost importance to me. Can you spend ten minutes of your time with me?"

"Sure, my boy. As I said you I am happy to help you. Come inside. Let us spend some time. I will do the best possible from my end."

I went inside and sat on the sofa. The Pundit asked me, "Can you now tell me what is the information you are looking for?"

"As I told you an hour back, when I extended my stay here, I happened to meet a person. That person helped me understand life and the way I can lead a happy and accomplished life."

The Pundit said, "That is really great. May I know the name of the person, so that I can talk to him too?"

"That is what I came here to ask you Punditji. I do not know his name. I spent a lot of time with him for the last three days. He never told me his name. I asked him many times. But, he was so firm not to disclose his name and identity. He promised me that he would tell me about his identity on the last day of my stay here, which is today. I came to collect the medicine after talking to him. I was supposed to know who he is, on my return. But, he was not there when I went to that place back after collecting the medicine."

"Tell me more. Tell me how he looked like and few other qualities that you noticed", probed the Pundit.

"He was in a brown robe. He had a lot of power in his eyes. He was extremely knowledgeable about life. He stayed in a hut on the mountains. He knew everything about me. He even knew about my dad, my wife and my son. Not just that. He knew even what I thought. He knew that I am not happy with my job. He knew that my dreams are different. He made me realize my Dharma. He made me realize my potential to fulfill my purpose of existence. He was an amazing guy."

"Tell me if he has told anything about his identity. Any clue . . . Where did he stay exactly?" the Pundit asked me. He seemed to be completely focused on getting to the answer I needed.

"He did not reveal anything. He must be a famous guy. When I asked him for the first time, he said that people called him the GURU. After that, there was no clue he left. Whenever I asked him, he told me that I will know on the last day of my stay here. He stayed in a hut on the mountain. The fifth trail on the right towards the mountains, and a hundred meters approximately from there would lead to his hut. What bewildered me is that the hut also is not there anymore. Further more surprising is that there is not even single evidence that a hut ever existed in that place."

The time was 6.40 PM.

The Pundit was silent for a while. I asked him, "Do you know the Guru? I am sure he would be a famous man. Please do not keep quiet. Please tell me who he is?"

"My boy, the mountain that you are talking about is not a place where people usually stay. There are a lot of stories that were built around that place. The ancient Siddhas, who stayed here, named it the MOUNTAIN OF ENLIGHTENMENT. It was a popular belief that people who go there get enlightened. But, of late, people do not believe it anymore. No one goes there either. What I mentioned is based on the ancient scriptures which I happened to read as a part of my research. It was elaborated that the mountain was also known as the mountain of reflections. This essentially meant that the power of that place made people reflect on their own self, study themselves and get enlightened. For years, people stopped going to that mountain as they are scared of the power, which they believed existed.

There is no one in this place called the GURU. No one as far as I am aware of, dares to stay there in that mountain.

I have been staying in this place for past 70 years. If there was anyone with that kind of powers, I would have known for sure."

I thanked the Pundit for his time and left.

I was on the flight back to my place. As I was thinking of what happened over the past three days, slowly I fell asleep. I heard the Guru's voice.

"My son, remember one thing in life. You are the only person who can teach you or change you. There is no one else who can do it for you. And there is no intelligence which is unavailable to you. When you really want something, the world will work for you. It will present you all the intelligence that it has, for you to pick whatever you want. There is nothing outside you. Everything is in you. What you choose is what will be available. What you believe is what you get. You are one with the Universe and there is no separation between you and the Universe. The Universe is just as how you want it to be. If you choose to see good, you see good. If you choose to see possibility, you see abundance of opportunities. If you want to live your dream, no one can stop you. There is nothing outside you. It is YOU who has to decide what you need to do. You will accomplish it beyond doubt, if you choose to accomplish it with conviction and belief. I am sure you will see this . . .

You have awakened my son. You are an ENLIGHTENED being now. Nothing can stop you.

Live your DHARMA. Fulfill your Purpose . . . THE WORLD WILL WORK FOR YOU."

CLOSURE NOTE

I reached home. Simone and Aarav were waiting eagerly for me. The first question that Simone and Aarav had for me was, "Who is the Guru? How is he?" I smiled and said, "His name is Svadhyaya Guru and he is a cool guy. He said that he will come whenever I wanted his help." I did not want to explain further details to Aarav. I decided to explain Simone at a later point of time. I saw Aarav and said, "Tomorrow morning 6 AM, we are on the beach". He hugged me with joy.

DHARMA was the name I chose for my Music recording Studio. It is an extremely successful Studio now. Dharma is a studio, fully based on the core values of my life. I drafted a plan for five years once I reached home back from India. I defeated all the hurdles in no time and reached my destiny within three and half years. The plan was perfect and was really challenging the possibilities. The belief was beyond. The execution of the plan was nothing less than excellent. Everything I visualized came true much before what I had planned in my journal.

I employ hundred and fifty people and I have 25 branches all across the world. Now, I am a fulfilled man living my dream, and living my statement of life.

I am doing WHAT I REALLY WANT TO DO in THE WAY THAT I WANT TO DO, ANYTIME and EVERYTIME.

I am living my DHARMA . . .

ABOUT THE AUTHOR

Vishnu Sharma was born in 1982, in Karnataka, a state in southern part of India. He completed his Bachelors in Engineering and Masters in Management. He is a spiritual seeker. In his quest to understand the deeper insights of spirituality, he discovered that the world is one with us. The happenings inside, change what happens in the world outside. Having experienced this beauty of inner world, he made it a vision of his life to help people realize the same. He is focused on helping people realize their dreams by changing their inner world. This book "the GURU who ROCKED my LIFE", is a mysterious tale embedded with powerful concepts, which are a result of his immense research on this subject.